ARCHANGELS DON'T PLAY PINBALL

BY DARIO FO

TRANSLATED BY RON JENKINS

S0-EBU-578

SAMUEL FRENCH, INC.

45 WEST 25TH STREET   NEW YORK 10010

7623 SUNSET BOULEVARD   HOLLYWOOD 90046

LONDON   TORONTO

Copyright © 1987, 1989 by Dario Fo and Ron Jenkins

ISBN 0 573 69140 1   Printed in U.S.A.

ARCHANGELS DON'T PLAY PINBALL had its American premiere at the American Repertory Theater in Cambridge, Massachusetts in June, 1987. It was directed by Dario Fo and Franca Rame. The cast was as follows:

TINY (SUNNY WEATHER)........Geoff Hoyle
FIRST FRIEND (Clerk, Dog Pound
    Director, Mayor).................. Peter Gerety
SECOND FRIEND (Clerk, Dog Catcher)
....Remo Airaldi
THIRD FRIEND (Clerk,
    Stationmaster) ....Benjamin Evett
FOURTH FRIEND (Jules, Bum, Sergeant,
    Illusionist)........................ John Bottoms
FIFTH FRIEND (Doctor, Clerk,
    Conductor).........................Dean Norris
PASTRY COOK (Coptic Priest, Inspector,
    General) ....Richard Grusin
BLONDIE ....Harriet Harris
FIRST GIRLFRIEND (Clerk, Woman at
    Dog Pound) .... Sally Schwager
SECOND GIRLFRIEND (Clerk, Dog
    Catcher).........................Alison Taylor
THIRD GIRLFRIEND (Woman at
    Window)....................Bonnie Zimering
FOURTH GIRLFRIEND (Second Woman
    at Window)....................... Rima Milla

TIME

Now

PLACE

Here

CHARACTERS

Tiny (Sunny Weather)
First Friend/Clerk/Dogcatcher/Policeman/
 Inauguration Participant
Second Friend/Clerk/Dog Pound Director/Mayor
Third Friend/Policeman/Detective/Magician/
 Town Official
Pastry Shop Owner/Priest/Man at Clerk's
 Window/Inspector/Senator
Fourth Friend/Clerk/Guard at Dog Pound/
 Stationmaster/Inauguration Participant
Fifth Friend/Doctor/Clerk/Conductor
Sixth Friend/Clerk/Policeman at Inauguration
First Woman Friend/Woman at the Clerk's
 Window/Woman Inauguration Participant
Second Woman Friend/Second Woman at
 Clerk's Window/Woman Inauguration
 Participant
Third Woman Friend/Woman Inauguration
 Participant
Blondie/Angela

ACT I

Scene 1

SCENE: The curtain is open. The stage is bare.

AT RISE: Seven young men appear UPSTAGE against a plain backdrop. They are dressed identically: black pants, striped suspenders, white shirts. Their steps keeping time to the music, they walk DOWNSTAGE as they sing.

THE NIGHT IS A BIG UMBRELLA, FULL OF
    HOLES
SOMEBODY'S SHOT IT UP WITH LEMON
    DROPS
THE MOON LOOKS LIKE A JACKPOT
    SPECIAL
FROM A GIANT PINBALL MACHINE FOR
    KING KONG

AND MY CITY IS ONE BIG PINBALL PARLOR
WITH GIRLS WHO ACT LIKE REPLAY
    FLIPPERS
AS SOON AS YOU TOUCH THEM THEY
    SCREAM OUT "TILT."
DON'T MOVE. DON'T TREMBLE.

7

DON'T LET IT TILT.
DON'T LET IT TILT.
YOUR EYES ARE GREEN FLASHERS
RED SPECIALS: SQUEEZE ME IF YOU WANT
    TO
DON'T LET IT TILT.
DON'T LET IT TILT.
THAT'S THE RULE OF THE GAME
A RULE THAT'S LITTLE KNOWN.
DON'T LET IT TILT.
DON'T LET IT TILT.
WE'RE A BIG GANG OF TOUGH GUYS
WE KIDNAP WEALTHY DOGS AND CATS
AND WHEN THEIR RICH OWNERS START
    CRYING
WE COLLECT A FAT RANSOM AND RUN

WE STEAL RADIOS FROM PARKED CARS
BUT CARS ARE LIKE FLIPPERS TOO
AS SOON AS YOU TOUCH THEM THEY
    SCREAM OUT TILT
YOU HAVE TO BE CAREFUL
DON'T LET IT TILT
DON'T LET IT TILT
GO EASY ON THE FLIPPERS
DON'T SET OFF THE ALARM
DON'T LET IT TILT
DON'T LET IT TILT
THERE'S NO NEED TO OVERDO IT
FLIP SOFTLY IF YOU WANT TO BE A CROOK

(*During the song a fence closes behind the young men. It runs the length of the stage and serves as a curtain. At the end of the song, one of the men, the smallest, lets himself go rigid and fall over. Two of his companions grab him under his armpits, and two others lift up his feet. The other two exit STAGE RIGHT.*)

TINY. Oooooooo!

FIRST: Dammit, you're heavy.

SECOND: Don't overdo it. You only have to look sick. Not dead!

TINY. And how do I do that?

THIRD. Get stiff.

TINY. Stiff like this? (*He arches his back.*)

FOURTH. Come off it. Stick in your stomach. (*Flattens him with a chop to the midsection.*)

TINY. (*Straightening up quickly.*) Hey. Take it easy. No, that's it. I quit. You can play the part of the stiff. I told you before, I don't like the idea, and I never did.

FIRST. Oh, you don't like it. Did you hear that? He never liked it. We're risking prison so he can get married in style. And this is the thanks we get.

THIRD. Come on. Do you expect gratitude from a wimp like him? You must have your head up your ass.

SECOND. We've all got our heads up our asses. We find him a wife with a nice ass and lots of money ... a virgin! ...

FOURTH. (*As if reading from a marriage announcement.*) From the best of families. Impeccable morals ... And now we're trying to get him a dowry, and he tells us he doesn't like playing the part of the stiff. What a louse.

THIRD. Aren't you ashamed of yourself?

TINY. (*Teary*-eyed.) Yes, yes. I'm ashamed and disgusted with myself. You're all so good to me. You always help me ... and what do I do ... I deserve to have someone spit in my eye. (*He spits in one of his companion's eyes.*)

FIRST. (*Cleaning the spit out of his eye.*) Hey, don't be so hard on yourself ... my eyesight's bad enough as it is.

(*The fence opens to reveal the interior of a pastry shop.*)

SECOND. Let's get on with it. Come on. Climb up.

TINY. Okay. I'm climbing. I'm climbing. (*He climbs onto his friend's back with both arms around his neck.*)

SECOND. Not like that ... on my shoulders.

TINY. I am on you shoulders: It's not my fault your neck is so low.

SECOND. Stop it.

TINY. Okay. I'm stopping. I'm stopping (*Moaning.*) Ohiii Ohiii Ohiii

(The SECOND FRIEND carries him on his back. The two others take his feet and they lift him into the shop entrance. The PROPRIETOR greets them. He is worried.)

PROPRIETOR. An accident? Was he run over?

SECOND. If it had only been a car ... a broken leg ... a little cast ... and he's be back on his feet ...

PROPRIETOR. Then, what is it? ...

(TINY is stretched out on the counter. He moans.)

THIRD. What is it? What is it? Can't you see he's dying.

(TINY groans.)

PROPRIETOR. And you carried him here to die in the store. On top of my cannolis.

SECOND. You'd rather we let him die in the middle of the street. Have you no heart?

PROPRIETOR. All right, then, call a doctor.

(TINY moans.)

THIRD. He's almost gone. Where's the telephone?

PROPRIETOR. Here ... Wait. I'll get the phone book ... Maybe it's better to call an ambulance.

FIRST. Give it to me. I think it's on the first page.

PROPRIETOR. (*Pointing to TINY.*) But, what's wrong with him?

(*TINY groans.*)

FOURTH. It must be a stomach seizure.

(*Enter one of the friends making a path for another who is carrying a doctor's bag.*)

FIFTH. Here's the doctor. I knew he'd need one. Make room.

DOCTOR. A chair, please.

(*Each one passes the order down the line with a quick turn of the head.*)

FIRST. A chair.
SECOND. A chair.
THIRD. A chair.
FOURTH. A chair.
FIFTH. A chair.
PROPRIETOR. A chair.

(*They pass chairs to one another so frantically that in the end all the chairs are back where they started and no one has succeeded in sitting down.)*

DOCTOR. (*To TINY.*) How do you feel?

TINY. (*Asking him.*) How do I feel?

DOCTOR. How should I know? (*In a low voice.*) You're supposed to tell me.

TINY. Oh, I'm supposed to say how I feel. But you all told me only to say, "ohi. ohi. ohi." ...

DOCTOR. (*Slaps him.*) Shut up.

TINY. Shut up. Ohi. Ohi. Ohi.

PROPRIETOR. (*Comes from behind the counter pushing aside TINY's friends.*) Doctor, what's wrong with him?

DOCTOR. (*Checking TINY's pulse.*) I can't believe he's still alive. He's got no pulse. (*Pushes TINY into a chair.*) May I?

TINY. Yes, you may?

DOCTOR. (*Puts his ear to TINY's back.*) Breathe. (*TINY takes a deep breath.*) Deeper. (*TINY obeys.*) Cough. (*TINY obeys.*) Louder.

(*The FRIENDS mimic the phony doctor by putting their ears against each other's backs in a chain staring with the first FRIEND's ear against the doctor's back. They react to each cough with successively larger responses as if the sound is getting louder at each point on the chain. *)

DOCTOR. Stick out your tongue. (*TINY obeys. The DOCTOR lifts up his eyelid.*) Bad. (*He shakes his head.*) Let's see your stomach. (*He pokes his stomach. TINY laughs as if he's being tickled.*) I knew it. Third degree food poisoning.

PROPRIETOR. Food poisoning. No. I'll bet it's just a broken romance.

THIRD. What kind of broken romance. He's getting married tomorrow morning.

PROPRIETOR. Then I was right.

TINY. (*Listening to his heart with a stethoscope he has slipped out of the DOCTOR's bag.*) It's going beep-beep-beep. (*Pointing to the stethoscope.*) The line must be busy. I'll call back later.

DOCTOR. (*Pulls it away from him.*) He must have eaten something rancid. Any of you know what it could be?

SECOND. We all had dinner together ... But he didn't eat anything. He was pre-occupied ... It was his last night of freedom.

DOCTOR. Are you sure he didn't eat anything?

FOURTH. Nothing at all. Just five or six cannolis that he picked up at some little joint ...

PROPRIETOR. (*Suddenly remembering.*) What do you mean, "some little joint." Now I know what he looks so familiar. He bought the cannolis here.

FIRST. So, he bought them here, did he?

SECOND. He did, did he? (*All surrounding the PROPRIETOR.*) Then you're the assassin.

PROPRIETOR. (*Backing up to the counter.*) Let's stop kidding around. You don't think it was my cannolis. We make them fresh every morning ... poison cannolis ... never in ten years ... and if you all ate them too ... that proves it!

FIFTH. It doesn't prove anything. Because none of us even tasted them. Fortunately, we didn't have time ...

ALL IN CHORUS: We were saved!

DOCTOR. (*Taking charge.*) Stop squawking and call an ambulance. Now! We can let the police take care of him.

FIRST. Here's the number. (*He dials, faking a call.*) Hello.

PROPRIETOR. (*Begging.*) Doctor, please. There must be some mistake. It couldn't have been my cannolis ...

DOCTOR. (*Cold and determined.*) Maybe not, but we'll have to turn it over to the Department of Public Health.

TINY. (*Loudly.*) Ohiohioau!

FIRST. (*With the phone in his hand.*) Damn. There's no answer. Where are they when you need them? Lazy bums!

(*One of the FRIENDS hits TINY to get another moan out of him.*)

TINY. Ohi ... ohi ... ohi!

SECOND. (*As if his heart is breaking.*) Doctor, can't you do something. An injection ... something. I can't stand seeing him in such pain.

TINY. Ohi ... ohi ... ohi. (*To his FRIEND.*) Pretty convincing, huh? Ohi ... ohi. .. ohi.

DOCTOR. (*Professional tone.*) I'm afraid it's too late for a stomach pump.

FOURTH. Well, if there's no hope ... maybe we should put him out of his misery. We could give him a few more of those cannolis and finish him off now. (*Picks up a pastry tray.*)

DOCTOR. Put down that pig food, and stop joking.

(*They all throw the cannoli around the room as if playing ball.*)

PROPRIETOR. (*Insulted.*) Wait a minute, doctor. Pig food? Let's not exaggerate. You'll see, when the health department examines my merchandise ...

FOURTH. They'll close down your shop. They'll suspend your license. And maybe they'll lock you up for life, dear mister baby-killer.

PROPRIETOR. Take it easy. and don't make any insinuations, because...

FIRST. Because? ... Because why? You call them insinuations, but everybody knows you make your pastries with ... artificial additives.

PROPRIETOR. (*Defensive.*) So what. Everybody uses them. Even the big chain bakeries.

DOCTOR. (*Like a referee.*) In any case, additives or no additives, the store will be closed during the investigation ... for a long time. So we'd better call the police immediately.

TINY. (*As if hallucinating.*) Yes, yes, the police. (*Picking up the phone.*) Hello, police ... send over a squad car ... (*He shouts as if he were an emergency siren.*)

DOCTOR. (*Grabbing the phone away from him.*) I should have called them sooner.

FIRST. Police? (*Thumbs through the pages of the phone book with incredible velocity.*) Here's the number. (*He dials.*)

TINY. (*Still hallucinating.*) Yes, yes. The police, and mommy too.

PROPRIETOR. (*Desperate.*) No. Please. Wait. You don't understand... If they close my shop, I'm finished. Have pity on me. I swear it's not my fault. Don't ruin me!

TINY. (*Playing the fool.*) Yes, yes. Ruin him. Ohi. Ohi. Ohi. I want my mommy!

DOCTOR. (*Understanding.*) You understand that as soon as we take him to the hospital, the doctors treating the poisoning would immediately report it to the police.

FOURTH. They'll take away your license forever.

PROPRIETOR. (*Crying.*) There's no hope. What can I do? (*The FOURTH FRIEND takes his hand consolingly.*) I put everything I have into this shop. And just when things were beginning to go well ... I could eat a ... (*He tries to bite his hand, but it is the one being held by the FOURTH FRIEND who ends up getting bit instead and shouts.*)

FIRST. Finally, the emergency number is ringing. Do you want to talk to them Doctor? (*Hands phone to DOCTOR.*)

FOURTH. Listen guys. (*Pulls out a handkerchief to wipe the sweat from the PROPRIETOR's face. He dries his tears and even blows his nose, then uses the dirty rag again on the man's face.*) I don't know if this man is honest or not, but let's give him the benefit of the doubt. We can't let him be thrown into the street on account of a little bad luck. He's not the one who makes the additives. The big manufacturers are to blame. It's the old story of big fish and little fish.

THIRD. Don't start with politics. Get to the point. What do you have in mind. You want us to throw our friend in the sewer to save this guy's shop?

TINY. No. Not the sewer. Mommeeeee!

SECOND. You, behave yourself, or we'll feed you another cannoli.

PROPRIETOR. (*Grabbing the phone from the hand of the phony doctor.*) Please, ... if you could

help ... sometimes a little good will is enough to
...

FOURTH. (*Distracted. Putting the phone to his ear*) What if we took him to some private clinic? Maybe they'd keep it quiet ... for a price.

DOCTOR. (*Takes the phone as if someone has just answered on the other end.*) Yes. But do you know how much it would take to cover up a case like this. A couple of thousand before you even walk in the door.

PROPRIETOR. (*Takes the phone.*) I could take care of that. Let's see how much cash I have. (*Puts down the phone and goes to the cash register.*)

FIRST. (*WInking.*) No. No. We couldn't do a thing like that. I'm all for helping my fellow man, but I don't want to go to jail for him. And if this one dies ... who wants that on their conscience?

THIRD. (*To TINY.*) Groan, stupid.

TINY. Yes, yes, I'm groaning ... ahiohiohi, how I'm groaning ... ohiohi ...

FIRST. Look, he's dying already.

FOURTH. Come on, don't be stingy. Have some compassion for this miserable wretch? (*He grabs a wad of bills from the PROPRIETOR's hand.*) Give me that. How much is there? (*Starts to count.*)

PROPRIETOR. Around two thousand. If you need more I could give you a check.

THIRD. No checks. The clinic we're taking him to doesn't accept them.

DOCTOR. (*Grabbing the money.*) That'll be enough for now. Then, we'll see ...

SECOND. Should we call a taxi?

DOCTOR. No, I've got my car outside. Let's go.

TINY. (*Begins to get up from the counter.*) Let's go, guys. (*A big slap sends him back down.*)

FOURTH. Be a good boy, now. (*Turning to the others.*) Give me a hand.

(*They lift LOFTY onto their shoulders.*)

PROPRIETOR. I don't know how to thank you ... I hope it all goes well.

DOCTOR. Don't worry. The director of the clinic is a close friend. But I think you better give me some of these cannolis to be analyzed. Once they're discovered the cause, it will be easier to prescribe the cure.

PROPRIETOR. Please, please, take them all. I was just going to throw them away ...

THIRD. We'll take care of them (*Grabbing armfuls of cannolis and cream puffs.*) We'll take these too. You never know.

(*One of the FRIENDS takes a pie.*)

PROPRIETOR. What do the pies have to do with it?

FOURTH. Pies are crucial. Pies are always crucial. (*Loads them up onto LUNGO's belly as if he were a serving tray.*)

SECOND. You have no idea how much material is required for a complete analysis. See you later.

PROPRIETOR. I hope not. (*He lets himself flop down into a chair.*) What a day. (*Without thinking he picks up a cannoli and takes a bite.*) What a close call. I'll never use artificial additives again ... You know you'd never guess from the taste of them that they're poisonous at all. ... Poisonous. (*He realizes that he's eaten half a cannoli.*) Oh, God, what have I done. Oh, God, I'm dying. Doctor, wait for me. (*He runs out of the store.*) Hey, you, wait for me. I'm coming too. (*Exits running.*) Oh, God, what have I done.

(*The fence curtain closes hiding the store. The gang enters. They laugh and slap each other with satisfaction.*)

FIRST. Ah. He really fell for it. What a turkey.

DOCTOR. You were all brilliant. I would have fallen for it myself...

TINY. Was I brilliant, too.

PROPRIETOR. Wait for me, stop ...

FOURTH. Looks like he's had second thoughts.

(*They slap TINY again, lift him up and leave. The PROPRIETOR enters.*)

PROPRIETOR. They're gone. Where are you? ... Wait for me, I don't want to die. (*He follows them the wrong way.*)

TINY. (*From opposite wing.*) Hey, Mr. Cannoli, we're over here. (*Exits chased by PROPRIETOR.*)

(*The gang re-enters.*)

FIRST. What a chase.

TINY. It was so beautiful.

THIRD. We lost him this take.

FOURTH. Yes, but let's get out of here and go to a bar. It'll be more peaceful.

(*The gang starts walking. Meanwhile on the left a table and chairs are carried on. On the chair, in the shadow, a man is seated. When the gang gets close, a light reveals him to be a gentleman who looks exactly like the pastry shop proprietor.*)

FIRST. Look, there he is again.

TINY. Let's go, guys. (*He lets himself stiffen and fall backwards, but this time there's no one to catch him. So he falls with a thud and stays on the ground without moving. The others bump into each other as they run away. One of them trips and falls.*)

GENTLEMAN. Hey, you guys. What's got into you? Andy, Bert ... have you gone crazy?

DOCTOR. (*Stopping suddenly.*) Michael, it's you. With that light from the side, I took you for the pastry shop owner. You know if you had an apron, you'd look just like him.

GENTLEMAN. What pastry shop owner?

(*One at a time the others in the gang re-enter.*)

FIRST. Hey, Michael, you really sent us for a loop.

THIRD and FOURTH. But who is it?

DOCTOR. Excuse me, these are my friends: Peter, Mark, Luke and Jules.

GANG. (*Introducing themselves.*) Nice to meet you, etc.

GENTLEMAN. (*Noticing the pastry tray.*) On you way to a party?

THIRD. We're coming back from one ...

DOCTOR. We just finished fleecing a pastry shop owner who could pass as your brother.

(*Meanwhile two of the friends approach TINY who has not moved since he fell down.*)

GENTLEMAN. Now I see why you were in such a hurry ...

SECOND. (*Poking TINY with his foot.*) Hey, Tiny, wake up. All clear.

FOURTH. We know you can play a great corpse, but you can stop now. (*He slaps him.*) Son of a bitch. He must have hit his head. Andy, come here. You're so good at playing doctor. Take a look at him.

(*The DOCTOR takes his pulse and heartbeat.*)

FIFTH. Acts like a real doctor.

DOCTOR. It's nothing. Throw a little water on his face and see what happens. Waiter, a pitcher of water please.

THIRD. I'll get some.

GENTLEMAN. Let's hope he doesn't have a concussion.

SECOND. Don't worry. Before you can have a concussion, you have to have a brain. He's got a head full of billiard balls.

DOCTOR. We only keep him around for laughs. We play tricks on him, and he falls for them every time. (*He goes to sit down on the only free chair, but one of the gang pulls it out from under him and he falls.*)

FOURTH. One time we made him believe he was invisible. (*One after another they pull the chair out from under each other – executed like a violent ballet, until finally the last friend thinks he has the chair to himself. It gets kicked out from under him, and he makes a theatrical fall. All this happens without interrupting the fourth friend's story.*) He fell for that one too: he walked down the street behind a woman and goosed her. The best part was that she liked it. But her boyfriend didn't. He was walking behind her and ... poor invisible man. He got two black eyes and couldn't see anything for days.

FIRST. But the best trick is the one we're playing on him now. We're marrying him to a streetwalker.

GENTLEMAN. To a what?

FOURTH. To a streetwalker, a woman who walks the streets.

SECOND. Well, she's not really a streetwalker, in the sense that she doesn't do it for a living. She's a part-timer.

FOURTH. Yes, she works at home (*Imitating a female voice.*) Are you ready, honey.

GENTLEMAN. But you're not going to marry them for real, are you?

DOCTOR. Are you crazy? Where would the fun be in that? ... Listen to what we did ... (*Turns to the FRIEND who's just arrived with the water.*) Wait. Let me tell him the story before you wake him up ... Then he can help us too ... (*Pointing to the GENTLEMAN.*) Okay, first we put the idea into his head ... telling him he had to find a wife, that he couldn't go on living like a bum his whole life ... like this ... like that ... etc. Then we made him take out a classified ad in the paper ...

FOURTH. Wait. He probably still has it in his pocket ... (*The first FRIEND goes through TINY's pockets and finds a scrap of old newspaper.*) There it is. Read it.

FIRST. (*Reading.*) "Unemployed youth, nondescript, mediocre appearance, slight physical defects ..."

FOURTH. We convinced him that it is always best to tell the truth.

FIRST. (*Continuing.*) "... would like to marry a young, rich, possibly blonde virgin. Good family background, without physical defects."

GENTLEMAN. And he actually went in person to place the ad? Imagine the clerk's face.

DOCTOR. Yes, but you should have seen his face, when the letter arrived that we had sent, pretending it was from a beautiful, rich Albanian.

GENTLEMAN. Why, Albanian?

FOURTH. So that we could invent an Albanian orthodox ritual which prohibited the groom from seeing the bride's face before the wedding.

THIRD. Imagine how much fun the wedding will be. We found a bride, and got the money to pay her and her friends from the pastry shop owner ...

THIRD. (*Pointing to the stolen goods.*) ...along with some nuptial pastries and pies.

FOURTH. We even have a holy robe (*Takes a black tunic from under his jacket.*) All we need is a coptic priest.

DOCTOR. But we have one now ... Look: there he is. (*Pointing to the gentleman.*)

GENTLEMAN. Me? You're crazy. A set-up like that. I couldn't do it. I'd burst out laughing.

FOURTH. You can do what you want. He'll never know the difference.

SECOND. Quiet, he's coming to.

TINY. (*Beginning to move his arms and bring his hands to his neck.*) Ahiohi, what a fall!

FIRST. Quick father, transform yourself.

(*From under his jacket he takes out the hat of an orthodox priest and puts it on his head. Another one helps him on with the black tunic. They lift him up onto the table where he sits on a chair as if it were a throne.*)

FOURTH. (*Slapping TINY.*) Come on, wake up. It's nothing. Just a nice nap.

TINY. And who's he ... Oh, it's you guys. (*Seeing the GENTLEMAN.*) Mr. Cannoli. Let's run. (*Starts to leave.*)

DOCTOR. No. Calm down. It's not the pastry shop owner. They look alike, but it's not him.

FOURTH. This is a coptic priest. We invited him especially for you.

TINY. A coptic, especially for me. (*He gets up slowly and walks over to the phony priest.*) A pleasure to meet you.

(*The THIRD FRIEND signals him to kneel.*)

FIRST. Kiss his hand, you pagan.

TINY. (*Kneeling.*) Yes, yes, excuse me and thank you for everything. (*Kisses his hand.*)

GENTLEMAN. Don't mention it. Rise my son, rise. (*Turns his head away so as not to laugh in TINY's face.*)

FIRST. Did you hear? Rise. That means pick him up and make him rise.

TINY. Pick him up? Why should I pick him up.

DOCTOR. It's an orthodox custom. Like here when the groom carries the bride over the threshold. In Albania the groom carries the bride's priest over the threshold ... Go ahead. Get moving. Lift him up on your shoulders. It's better.

TINY. The bride's priest on my shoulders? Where should I take him.

FOURTH. To the bride's house. Where else? Come and we'll show you the way.

(*A red tablecloth has been placed over the table which the friends lift up over the GENTLEMAN's head as it it were a papal canopy.*)

TINY. Good, good. Finally I get to see her.
FOURTH. Now, sing.

(*They form a procession as they sing: "The night
is a big umbrella full of wholes, someone has
shot it up with lemon drops."*)

BLACKOUT

(*As they leave the fence opens.*)

ACT I

Scene 2

*Inside the girl's house. Paper party decorations.
The phony priest ties TINY's wrists to the
wrists of his bride. TINY is blindfolded and
his bride is dressed in white with a veil hiding
her face. Three girls and the gang stand in
chorus, each with a candle in hand, singing:*

SQUEEZE MY WRISTS
TIGHT AGAINST YOURS,
EVEN WITH MY EYES SHUT
I CAN SEE YOUR EYES.
PLEASE TAKE MY LOVE
I'LL GIVE IT FOR A SMILE.
SQUEEZE MY WRISTS

TIGHT AGAINST YOURS
EVEN WITH MY EYES SHUT
I CAN SEE YOUR HEART.

PRIEST. (*Steps between the bride and groom.*)
Repeat after me, but not out loud: Whatever your
virtues, whatever your flaws, I will honor and
keep you 'till death do us part.

CHORUS. 'till death do us part.

PRIEST. Forever close, not that fate has
brought you to me.

CHORUS. 'till death do us part.

PRIEST. From now on, my shadow will be
your shadow, I will see light through your eyes,
and I will speak with your mouth.

CHORUS. 'till death do us part.

PRIEST. My blood will flow through your
heart, and yours through mine. We will be one till
death do us part.

CHORUS. 'till death do us part.

PRIEST. You are man and wife ... You may
now see each other.

(*Two FRIENDS untie them and remove the
blindfolds. First TINY, then the bride, a tiny
blonde with an incredibly pure face. Everyone
applauds. Then there is silence. The bride
smiles and TINY is dumbfounded and still.*)

TINY. Oheuuu.

DOCTOR. Is that all you can say? How do you like her?

TINY. Oheuuu.

BRIDE. It's a pleasure to meet you.

TINY. A pleasure. Oheuuu.

THIRD. Say something. After all, she's your wife.

TINY. Is it true, she's my wife?

CHORUS: Yes, you just married her.

TINY. Oheuuuu. A pleasure.

BRIDE. (*With simplicity.*) A pleasure.

PRIEST. And you, miss ... I mean Mrs... I just married you ... I was saying, how do you like your husband.

BRIDE. He's wonderfully tiny ... Oheuuu, so tiny. He's the tiniest.

TWO OF THEM IN CHORUS. Oheuuu. A pleasure.

DOCTOR. Ah, what a beautiful couple. Long live marriage.

ALL. Hallelujah.

THIRD. Come on. Come on. The groom pours the drinks.

TINY. (*Grabbing a bottle while the girls get trays of food.*) Listen, Jules, you're sure this isn't a joke ...

JULES. A joke? You must be joking. Do we look like jokers?

TINY. No, but what if she changes her mind?

JULES. Don't worry, she won't change her mind ... She never had a mind. How can she change it?

TINY. No mind? But she's beautiful, oheuuu. Ehiii... (*The whole gang is kissing the bride and her friend.*) Me, too. I want to kiss the bride, she's my bride ... (*He can't get to her in the crowd. The men in the gang pass her back and forth to one another as if playing a kissing game, and the girls play along, allowing themselves to be kissed and hugged. There is spinning, shouting and laughter, until gradually they all disappear through the wings. TINY is left holding the orthodox PRIEST.*) She's my bride ...

PRIEST. What are you doing? I'm the priest.

TINY. The priest. It's a pleasure to meet you. (*Kisses his hand.*) Excuse me, but I wanted to kiss the bride. Where is she?

PRIEST. Probably in some bedroom with one of your friends.

TINY. Oh, I see ... (*As if struck by lightning.*) In some bedroom?! In bed?

PRIEST. Yes, it's an old orthodox custom. Here you kiss the bride, but in Albania you go to bed with her. It's the custom. (*Suddenly there are loud voices offstage.*)

BLONDIE. Creep! Take it off. Take it off, now!

VOICE. What's the matter? ... Ohi. Get your hands off me ...

BLONDIE. It's not yours. You've no right to ruin it like that.

DOCTOR. (*Enters wearing BLONDIE's white dress. BLONDIE is behind him in her slip.*) All right, I'll take it off. I was only joking.

BLONDIE. And be careful not to rip it.

(*Another friend enters wearing the dress of one of the girls. Then another and another. All in drag.*)

FIRST TRANSVESTITE. (*While the GIRLS giggle stupidly.*) Calm down, girls. This is serious. Let's get on with it.

SECOND. (*Also in drag turns to TINY.*) What a beautiful hunk of a man. Too bad he's married, otherwise ... I'd do something wild.

THIRD. (*Pointing to a FRIEND he has in his arms.*) Please, Mr. Priest, we want to get married.

FOURTH. Yes, we want to legalize our relationship. Until now we've been living in sin.

BLONDIE. You make me sick. Out. All of you.

DOCTOR. But, Blondie, we made a deal.

BLONDIE. We made a deal that you wouldn't wreck the place.

A GIRL. But they didn't do anything.

ANOTHER GIRL. What's the big deal. It's only a night gown.

BLONDIE. But it's a real night gown. I sleep with that nightgown.

DOCTOR. With only the nightgown?

(*ALL laugh.*)

BLONDIE. (*turning to the GIRLS.*) And if you don't like it, you can leave too. Get out.

GIRLS. Okay, we're going. A little edgy, aren't you ... what a drag ... Goodbye... Let's go to my house where you can wear all the women's clothes you want.

FOURTH. The only parties you remember are the ones that end badly. Goodbye, dear.

FIRST. And to think that this joke cost a thousand bucks. I'm still not sure who the fool is, him or us.

BLONDIE. (*Turning to the PRIEST, who is chanting.*) You, too, your holiness, get lost.

PRIEST. (*Going towards the door.*) Be happy, my child. (*She blows him a raspberry. The PRIEST answers referring to her elegant style.*) Oh, a Radcliffe girl! (*He leaves.*)

BLONDIE. Drop dead ... (*Closes the door.*) Finally, they're gone. I couldn't have stood another minute.

TINY. (*Seated upstage.*) They got a little carried away.

BLONDIE. (*Without thinking.*) You call that "little."

TINY. Once they get started, they don't know when to stop ... then somebody always gets hurt ...

BLONDIE. (*Stops herself.*) Hey, what are you doing here. I thought you left with the others.

TINY. (*Bluntly.*) But why would I want to. We're newlyweds, and it wouldn't be right for me to leave you on the first night. It just wouldn't be right.

BLONDIE. (*Runs to window, leans out and shouts.*) Hey, you forgot something.

VOICE FROM OUTSIDE. Oh, yeah, Tiny. He's a gift from heaven. Enjoy him ... (*Laughs.*) Good night, lovebirds.

BLONDIE. Bastards! ... And now, what can I say?

TINY. (*Without irony.*) Tell me about yourself: what you were like as a child.

BLONDIE. What?

TINY. (*Still with candid sincerity.*) If we want to get to know each other, it might be best to start with our childhoods. For example, I remember being so mature as a child that at the age of fifteen, people took me for ten.

BLONDIE. And I remember being so mature as a child that at the age of fifteen they took me for five.

TINY. No. So young?

BLONDIE. Five dollars. Cash.

TINY. (*Laughs, then changes attitude.*) Don't act tough with me. I can see through it. I felt you tremble when your wrists touched mine, like that

... (*He comes close to her and re-assumes the position of the ritual.*) Admit it, you were getting emotional.

BLONDIE. Well, a little emotional, sure ... What am I saying? (*She starts to take down the party decorations. TINY gives her a hand.*) Everybody was singing ... all those words: "my shadow will be your shadow ... my blood will flow through your heart..." Uhei! That stuff has an effect! ... And the white dress ... Dammit, I bet if you put a white dress on an elephant, she'd get goosebumps too. It was the situation that got me all worked up ... not you ... or anybody else.

TINY. Me or anybody else? But what about when you said: oheuuu, you're so tiny ...

BLONDIE. I just said you were tiny, that's all. You are tiny, aren't you?

TINY. Yes, but when you said I was tiny ... it didn't have anything to do with tininess ... nobody ever told me I was tiny like that before ... say it again.

BLONDIE. That you're tiny.

TINY. Yes, I like the way you say it.

BLONDIE. Now, you're making fun of me? Don't you ever ... (*She throws some of the decorations at him which he catches calmly.*)

TINY. Me, make fun of you? Never. You're too beautiful. And pretty tiny yourself ... And for you I'd like to be even tinier ... teeny weeny tiny tiny ... So tiny that you'd say, "Oh, you're the tiniest."

BLONDIE. (*Angry and flattered at the same time.*) Come on, let's stop. When I hear you talk like that, I feel like I'm in a madhouse. They told me you were a little unbalanced, but I had no idea ... (*She walks towards him maternally.*) Is it possible that after all this, it still hasn't dawned on you that your friends ...

TINY. (*Without taking in what she said, worried.*) Speaking of my friends, that custom about everyone sleeping with the bride ... does it still go on after the first day ...

BLONDIE. What are you talking about? What custom?

TINY. (*Almost talking to himself.*) No, because it might start getting on your nerves, if someone was sitting quietly at home with his wife, and a friend came in and said, "Excuse me, could I borrow her for a while. I want to try out the custom again." (*Firmly to the GIRL who is looking at him with a stunned expression.*) I'm sorry to have to say this, but it's better to make things clear from the start ... call me old-fashioned, call me conservative, but I don't like it at all.

BLONDIE. What did they tell you? (*With angry gestures she picks up the glasses from around the room.*) How did I ever get myself mixed up in this farce. How the hell could anyone enjoy making fun of someone like you. It's an out and out disgrace. What fun is it to hit someone over the head if they're only going to smile at you and say thanks. Or to spit in someone's face and have them just stand there and look at you, the way you're looking now.

TINY. (*Maintaining an unchanging melancholy smile.*) What's wrong with my face? Is it ugly?

BLONDIE. Of course not. It is a little stupid looking, but at least it's honest.

TINY. Yours is honest too.

BLONDIE. (*She looks at him, beginning to smile, but suddenly becoming cold.*) Shouldn't you be leaving? I'd like to be left in peace.

TINY. (*Gets up reluctantly, stretching out his words.*) Okay, I'm going ... but calm down. It wasn't a total loss. In fact, you were paid rather well, (*Suddenly evil.*) And now your conscience is bothering you, because you earned your money at the expense of a poor idiot who stands there looking at you as if you were Snow White with her seven dwarfs. So you start yelling and raving ... Calm down, okay. (*The GIRL is speechless.*) Calm? ... Goodnight. (*Begins to leave.*)

BLONDIE. Wait ... You're not going to tell me that all of a sudden your brain has started working?

TINY. (*Comes back a few steps, and leans against a chair, still looking at her with his melancholy smile.*) Don't worry. My brain has been working all along. I know they make fun of me. In fact I'm usually the one who sets up the joke in the first place. They don't have much imagination, and if I didn't help them out, they wouldn't come up with much on their own.

BLONDIE. (*Lets herself fall into a chair, astonished.*) What kind of fool are you? Not only do they make fun of you, but you help them. Why?

TINY. (*Takes a cigarette out of his pocket.*) For me playing the fool is something of a profession.

BLONDIE. You're a professional fool?

TINY. Did you ever hear of a court jester. (*Lights his cigarette.*)

BLONDIE. Of course I've heard of them. (*Erudite, encyclopedic.*) Court Jesters were employed to evoke the laughter of kings ... right?

TINY. (*Laughing.*) Absolutely. It's the same with me. The only difference is that they don't have kings anymore. So I evoke laughter from my friends at the cafe. I'm a poor man's Rigoletto. But the important thing is, that it earns me a living.

BLONDIE. (*Incredulous.*) They give you a salary?

TINY. I earn more than I would if I were a clerk, and I work a lot less. Look. Everything I'm wearing, they've given me. I sleep at their houses. They pay for my food, wine cigarettes. And if I ask for a loan, they never turn me down. No one refuses to lend money to a fool.

BLONDIE. (*Spits on the ground in contempt.*) What kind of a man are you. Doesn't it disgust you to earn a living that way?

TINY. (*In the same tone, provoking her.*)
How does it make you feel to earn a living in that
other way?

BLONDIE. (*After a moment of silence.*)
Bull's-eye.

TINY. (*Expecting another reaction,
saddened.*) Excuse me, it slipped out.

BLONDIE. (*Melancholy, sighing.*) No, I
deserved it. Me who makes a profit on love itself.
It's enough to make you die laughing. But the idea
of it makes me angry. A woman can disguise the
way she earns her money, but in the end it comes
down to the same thing. But for a man ...

TINY. (*Gets up, carries his chair close to her
and sits down.*) It's the same thing. It all depends
on how you begin ... Someone like you doesn't
decide one day how to make a living. Either
you're born into it, or you ease your way in slowly.
Me, I was born into it. It started with my father.
His last name was Weather, so for a little joke, he
baptized me with three names: Sunny, Cloudy and
Stormy. "This way he can choose for himself
according to the atmospheric conditions," he said.

BLONDIE. (*Laughing, then she stops,
embarrassed.*) Ah, what a fool.

TINY. (*Getting louder.*) Yes, already a fool.
Imagine what it was like with my friends at
school ... "How are you", "What's the weather
forecast today" ... for years and years.

BLONDIE. (*Without smiling.*) It must have
been awful.

TINY. (*Relaxed, like a storyteller talking about something that happened to someone else.*) Ever the war made fun of me ... Soldiers get wounded everywhere, I know ... in the arm ... in the leg ... even the head ... But I got shot in the coccyx. A bullet knocked it clean away. Zac. Trach.

BLONDIE. (*Unable to control herself, explodes into laughter.*) Ah. (*Giggles.*) Ihp ... But how is it possible that you got hit right there ... ihp.

TINY. You see. "How is it possible" ... You're laughing so hard, it's giving you the hiccups. Even Fate found it entertaining to shoot me in precisely that spot.

BLONDIE. Ah. Ah.

TINY. I was discharged as a partially disable veteran, and now I'm eligible for special benefits, privileges, and even a pension. One day I was sitting on a trolley and a guy asked me to give him my seat. "I'm a disabled veteran," he said. "I'm disabled, too," I answered. He looked at me in disbelief and asked, "Where?" "In the coccyx," I said. Before I could finish speaking, he pulled me up by my tie and shouted, "Listen, I've got nothing against homosexuals, but I can't stand people who go around bragging about it." He was ready to throw me through the window. (*The GIRL laughs.*) And you wonder how I wound up playing Rigoletto.

BLONDIE. (*Affectionately.*) Excuse me for saying so, but you bring it on yourself. Anyone who walks with his head turned round to listen for people talking about him behind his back is bound to bump into the nearest lamp-post. Sbang. ihp. (*She hiccups.*) Then he curses fate for planting lamp-posts on sidewalks.

TINY. Congratulations. This time you hit the bull's-eye. ... But may I ask how you can be so accurate in assessing the flaws of others, mine in particular, and still let yourself be trapped in the kind of life you live.

BLONDIE. (*Takes a tray and speaks in staccato.*) Because when I began, I was more ignorant than now. And ignorance is the worst flaw of all. My father always said ... ihp ... (*Hiccups, then repeats the phrase with the cadence of a broken record.*) My father always said ... ihp ... my father always said ... (*This happens as she is wiping a tray, moving her hand as if it were the arm of a gramophone needle. TINY lifts up her arm, then puts it back on the tray as if he were adjusting the needle on a broken record. The GIRL continues speaking as if nothing had happened.*) My father always said that if a man or a woman was afflicted with ignorance, they would turn out like plants without leaves: empty poles. Even as a pole, I'm a twisted specimen.

TINY. (*Smiling sympathetically, without looking at her.*) Well, sometimes you're better off being twisted, if you happen to find another pole who's twisted in the opposite direction ... If you tie them together at the top... (*Takes a breath.*) ... the two of them would stand up stronger than if they were straight.

BLONDIE. (*Takes a step to observe him better.*) Is there a double meaning to that? (*Hiccups.*) Are you talking about us?

TINY. (*Stands up slowly, speaking erratically.*) Why don't we pretend, that we don't know: me, who you are: you, who I am ... Tell me ... would you want to, stay with me?

BLONDIE. (*Speeding up the rhythm. Slowing down at the end.*) Stay with you? How? ... Just for tonight, or for a long, long time. No, because if it was only a night, I'd tell you who I am, and you'd have to pay my fee.

TINY. (*Sits down again, rubbing his hands together.*) We're not laughing anymore.

BLONDIE. (*With intensity, almost falsetto.*) What did you expect? ... Don't you see that I'm telling you all this because I think I understand you, and because, God knows, I never get a chance to explain things like this to anyone?

(*Knock at the door.*)

FRIEND. (*From outside.*) Anybody home?

BLONDIE. Ihp ... (*Hiccups.*) Go away. I'm busy.

FRIEND. Let me in. I brought back your clothes.

BLONDIE. Okay. (*Opens the door.*) Come in. Let's see ... You've made a mess of them.

FRIEND. (*Noticing TINY.*) Oh. So he's still here? (*Swaggers.*) I'll get rid of him for you? (*Speaks to TINY with undisguised irony.*) Excuse us, Tiny. I have to speak to the lady about a delicate subject. Would you please get your ass out of here.

(*TINY doesn't move. The GIRL throws the clothes violently down on a chair.*)

BLONDIE. His ass is staying right here. If anybody's ass is leaving, it's yours.

FRIEND. (*Trying to avoid her as she advances threateningly.*) You don't understand ... I'm not here to waste your time ... I'm a paying customer ... Cash in advance... Look ... (*Shows her a roll of bills.*) Just like a bunch of roses. Come on. Throw him out. Tonight, there's poetry in my soul.

BLONDIE. (*Looks for a moment at TINY who is still sitting, distracted as if his mind was elsewhere.*) I'm throwing you out! And now I'm going to put away these clothes. (*Whispers to TINY as she leaves.*) Come on, show me if you're really interested in a twisted pole.

(*The FRIEND has taken off his jacket.*)

FRIEND. (*Turns to TINY with firm resolve.*) Now, listen ... and try to get it into your fat head ... (*Throws his jacket on a chair.*)

TINY. (*Stands as if he's just woken up.*) Okay. I get it. I'm leaving...

FRIEND. (*Surprised.*) You're leaving?

TINY. (*Turning back.*) Why, don't you want me to?

FRIEND. No ... no...

TINY. (*Sits down again.*) Then I'll stay.

FRIEND. No ... no ..! I meant: yes, yes ...

TINY. (*Gets up again, perturbed.*) Yes, yes or no, no? You seem to be a little mixed up. (*Sits down again.*) In any case, you'll have to lend me fifty dollars for a taxi ...

FRIEND. (*Reaches automatically into his jacket on the chair.*) Fifty dollars? ... Where are you going?

TINY. To the central police station. It's the only one that's still open.

FRIEND. (*He turns around suddenly.*) Police station ? ... What for?

TINY. (*Casually crossing his legs.*) To report a few minor incidents: like fraud and blackmail at the pastry shop ... my conscience is bothering me ... the more I think about it the more I'm convinced I should turn myself in ... Now that I'm married, I've decided to reform.

FRIEND. (*Shocked, then becoming more aggressive.*) What's gotten into your head? ... Do you want to get us all locked up ... I'll strangle you. You ungrateful skunk. And after all we've done for you.

TINY. (*Feigning shock.*) Only for me? ... And who is this for? (*Pointing to the money.*)

FRIEND. What do you care? That's for our trouble. We have to eat, too, pal.

TINY. (*Bored, stretches out his legs.*) Of course, you have to eat. On second thought, maybe I shouldn't turn myself in. I'd end up in jail, too...

FRIEND. (*Relieved.*) And they'd keep you in longer than all the rest of us put together.

TINY. (*Casual again, smiling, accompanying his words with small gestures. His head tilts expressively from one side to another.*) No longer than you. No. I'm a fool ... everyone knows I'm a fool ... I could always say your forced me into it ... that I really believed I was poisoned. If you can make someone believe he's invisible and married to a whore, you can make him believe anything. In fact, the judge might even give you a few extra months for taking advantage of a helpless fool.

FRIEND. (*After a pause, he takes his hands out of his pockets and approaches TINY in amazement.*) What's going on? ... Is that you talking, or some brother of yours with a Harvard degree that you've been hiding in the closet? So you were only playing the fool to get a free ride at our expense. Son of a bitch. And we thought you were just a clown.

TINY. (*With an insolent smile.*) Yeah. Life is strange that way. You think one thing, and on the contrary ... This money for example (*Points to*

the money that came out of the FRIEND's pocket.)
You thought it was yours, and now ... it's mine.
(Takes it.)

FRIEND. Give me that money ... or I'll break
your face. *(Grabs TINY and lifts him to his feet.)*

TINY. There's something else I forgot to tell
you ... I have a mean right hook *(He punches him
and kicks him out the door.)* Out. Out.

FRIEND. You'll pay for this, Tiny. You won't
be talking so big when the rest of the gang finds
out about this.

(BLONDIE returns.)

BLONDIE. Ihp. *(Hiccups.)* He's right. They
won't let you get away with that. Goodbye court
jester ...

TINY. If I was worried about that, I would
never have made the mistake of telling you about
myself.

BLONDIE. Ihp. *(Hiccups.)*

TINY. Why don't you try drinking from the
wrong side of the glass. Maybe it will cure your
hiccups.

BLONDIE. What?

TINY. Like this, look. *(He takes a glass of
water, bends over and tries to drink from the
opposite side of it. The water spills all over him
and he coughs.)* I was saying that maybe it was a
mistake to start telling you all about me. Maybe I
should have left things as they were.

BLONDIE. (*Tries the trick with the glass. Takes a deep breath*) Ah. I'm cured.

TINY. That's great ... ihp ... (*He hiccups.*) Now I've got them.

BLONDIE. I'm sorry ... what were you saying about leaving things as they were.

TINY. I was saying that if I'd left things as they were, maybe I wouldn't be leaving empty-handed.

BLONDIE. You're leaving? (*TINY nods his head.*) But where will you go?

TINY. I've got enough here for a hotel. (*Indicates they money he took from the friend.*) And maybe even enough to get to Washington. (*Hiccups.*)

BLONDIE. Washington?

TINY. Yes, I want to see if I can get some of my pension money. Then it'll be easier to walk down the street without turning my head around, as you put it. (*Hiccups.*) Bye. It's been a pleasure. (*Holds out his hand.*)

BLONDIE. (*Slowly, almost embarrassed, she gives him her hand.*) Bye. A pleasure.

TINY. A pleasure, what?

BLONDIE. What do you mean, a pleasure what?

TINY. (*Lecturing.*) When you say, "it's been a pleasure," you're supposed to give your name. What's your name?

BLONDIE. Angela.

TINY. Ihp. (*Hiccups.*) Angela?

BLONDIE. (*Taking his hand tenderly.*) Yes
... well, my real name is Angelica ... But you
know, in my profession ... being called angelic
would be a little silly. I guess when they baptized
me, the never imagined ...

TINY. No ... anyway, Angela's more
beautiful. (*Smiles. Tilts his head.*) Goodbye,
Angela. We'll meet again. (*Hiccups.*)

BLONDIE. Goodbye ... we'll meet again, eh?
Be careful. There's no light on the stairs.

TINY. Don't worry. I can see fine.

BLONDIE. Goodbye. (*A crashing sound
offstage.*) What happened?

TINY. (*From offstage, trying to restrain
himself from cursing.*) Dammit. You were right.
I really do have this problem of walking around
with my head turned backwards. I didn't see the
steps.

BLONDIE. Did you hurt yourself?

TINY. (*Offstage.*) No. It's nothing.

BLONDIE. Did it cure your hiccups?

TINY. (*Offstage.*) Let's hope so.

BLONDIE. Goodbye.

TINY. Goodbye, Angela. We'll meet again.

BLONDIE. Wait. Wait.

TINY. (*Offstage, with a note of hope in his
voice.*) Yes?!

BLONDIE. I have to tell you something. Uh ...
what should I call you? I mean, which of your
names do you prefer?

TINY. (*A brief pause indicating disappointment, then he answers euphorically.*) Call me Sunny ... because after tonight, I can be happy my father gave me that name.

BLONDIE. Goodbye, Sunny.

TINY. Goodbye, Angela.

(*Prolonged noise of someone falling down the steps.*)

BLONDIE. If that doesn't cure your hiccups, nothing will. (*She laughs. Take a transistor radio. Turns it on and hangs it around the neck of a tailor's dummy that's in the center of the room. We hear faintly the song, "Squeeze My Wrists Tight,"*) Sunny ... Tiny Sunnyweather... He's right: it brings on the urge to make puns... (*She sings along with the music from the radio. She looks out through the window curtains. Slowly she starts to get undressed, kicking one shoe up in the air.*) "Squeeze my wrists tight." (*She picks up a jacket that was forgotten on the chair. Without thinking she puts it on the mannequin. She lifts up the mannequin and mimes a passionate embrace. Only now does she realize the jacket belongs to TINY.*) This belongs to Sunny ... What do you know ... I sent him out in the cold with no jacket ... now he has to come back ... he can't go to Washington without his jacket ... he'll be back for sure ... and when he come in I'll say, "Sunny, dear, if you want to wear your jacket, you'll have to wear me too." (*Tries to imitate TINY's voice.*) "But, you already said no." "And now I say yes ... I changed my mind. I think I could be very happy with a twisted pole like you ..." (*Embraces the mannequin again.*) Come here, come here close to me. Come on, don't tremble like that ... Oheuuu, my heart's beating like crazy ... And yours? (*She puts her ear to the mannequin's chest. Someone starts knocking at the door.*) Stop exaggerating. (*She realizes the sound is the door.*) It's you. You came back to get your jacket. Come in. (*She realizes she's undressed.*) ... No, wait. Don't come in. (*She hides behind a screen.*) Okay. You can come in now. (*The FRIEND enters.*) But don't come here. Excuse me if I made you wait, but I was undressed ... I know it's silly of me to want to hide myself ... I'm not usually so proper ... I don't know why... When I'm with you I get shy ... It's stupid, but that's how I feel ... I've already said and done a lot of stupid things today ...

FRIEND. (*Flattered.*) Well ...

BLONDIE. No ... don't say anything ... other wise I won't have heart to tell you the things I've got to tell you, if not I'll just burst... I've got a crush on you ... Don't laugh ... I've really (*The FRIEND is feeling like a king.*) I didn't realize it until you had gone, and I found myself talking to your jacket, "I hope he comes back to get you, then he'll have to take me too." Oh, now I've done it ... (*Laughs.*) Aren't you going to say something? ... I knew you'd be surprised ... It wasn't easy for me either, to tell you that, but now I'm glad I said it. (*Comes out from behind the screen.*) Here I am ... (*The GIRL is shocked to see the FRIEND. He smiles happily.*)

FRIEND. (*He comes towards her on his toes, walking like a horny rooster.*) Damn. I'm a wizard. I put a spell on you. And I thought you didn't even like me. Funny how you get it all wrong, sometimes (*He caresses her.*) And now you'll see that you made the right choice. (*The GIRL doesn't move.*) What's the matter, did the look in my eyes turn you to stone? Come on, beautiful. (*He slaps her gently.*) Wake up, and I'll take you to bed.

BLONDIE. (*Responds by giving him a big slap.*) Out. (*She throws everything she can find at him.*) Out. Out. Out.

FRIEND. Okay, I'm going. I'm going. You don't have to ... Take it easy.

(*He exits and there is the sound of another big crash on the stairs. Crying, the GIRL goes to the mannequin, looks at it for a moment, then kicks it over onto the ground. The radio that was around its neck falls to the ground. Concerned, the GIRL picks it up, turns it on, and shakes it, hoping it isn't broken The radio is still working. An announcer's voice is heard saying:*)

RADIO ANNOUNCER. ... Most of the region will enjoy sunny weather. This has been a report on atmospheric conditions. Our next broadcast will be at one o'clock tomorrow.

(*The GIRL bursts into tears and smashes the radio onto the ground.*)

ACT II

Scene 1

NTS Black tailcoats, with clown wigs adorned with bright clumps of hair making a semicircle from one temple to the other. They wear rubber stamps around their necks. They parade in front of a partition made up of window stations. They march towards the audience singing:

TO GIVE GLORY TO CHEOPS THEY MADE HIM A PYRAMID

AN ALTAR TO LEONIDAS, AND CEASAR GOT AN ARCH,

FOR VERCINGETORIX A MONOLITHIC OBELISK,

IN MEMORY OF A SAILOR, THEY BAPTIZED AMERICA, THE CONTINENT DISCOVERED BY COLUMBUS,

THEY CHRISTEN MICROBES WITH THE NAMES OF DOCTORS AND SCIENTISTS

WHO WANT TO BE IMMORTALIZED

SHORT OF PYRAMIDS, HAVE GIVEN THEIR NAMES TO ORGANS

THERE'S BERIO'S BONE, AND THE
    EUSTACHIAN TUBE
THERE'S BARIO'S NERVE, AND SCIPIO'S
    HELMET
THERE'S DARIO'S CHARIOT, AND A
    MONUMENT FOR EACH
BUT NOBODY REMEMBERS WHO THOUGHT
    OF IT ALL.

WHO WAS THE GREAT BUREAUCRAT WHO
    INVENTED FORMS IN TRIPLICATE

TRANSIT PAPERS, AND VERIFICATION
    STAMPS
UNPERMISSABLE PRACTICES, AND
    ADDITIONAL TAXATION
INVALIDATED SIGNATURES, CERTIFI-
    CATES OF DISCHARGE
HONORARY DISCHARGES, OBLIGATORY
    GRATUITIES COMMON PROTOCOL,
    CERTIFIED BONDS?
NO STONE RECORDS HIS DATE OF BIRTH
PERHAPS HIS FILE'S LABELLED
    "ANONYMOUS" "ANONYMOUS"

BROTHERS OF THE OFFICE. LET US RAISE
    OUR HEADS
LET'S SING TO THE SPIRIT OF RE-USABLE
    RUBBER STAMPS

OPEN UP OUR WINDOWS AND PRAISE THE
    LORD
WHO LOVES US ENOUGH TO HELP US KEEP
    IN STOCK:
OFFICIAL SEALS AND BONDED PAPER
POSTAGE STAMPS AND PRE-ADDRESSED
    STATIONERY
THE DOORKEEPER, THE PEN AND PENCIL
    HOLDER,
AND CIRCULAR FILES FOR DEPARTMENT
    SUPERVISORS

(*The five clerks take their places behind their
service windows. During the song all
windows were open. Now they're all closed
except one. A woman enters, goes to the first
window, and quickly takes care of some
business. TINY enters. He's carrying a
heavy suitcase and a package. He gets in line
behind the woman. When his turn comes the
window shuts, as another window opens.
TINY, weighed down with his suitcase and
package, but above all distracted by the
strange resemblance between the woman and
one of Angela's friends, is late getting to the
open window. Consequently he arrives there
after a gentleman who has just walked in.*)

TINY. Excuse me, but I was here first ... If it
were just a matter of running, there'd be no need
for lines.

GENTLEMAN. I wasn't running.

TINY. (*Noticing a strange resemblance between the man and one of his friends.*) It's the coptic priest ... What are you doing here in Washington?

GENTLEMAN. I beg your pardon?

TINY. Come on. Stop joking. I recognize you, even with the moustache.

GENTLEMAN. It's you who should stop joking ... especially with those who have neither time nor desire.

TINY. Excuse me, but I mistook you for one of my friends who doesn't have a moustache ... In any case, since you do have a moustache, I'd advise you to hold onto it ... Okay? ... Still friends?

(*At that moment another window opens.*)

GENTLEMAN. Listen, my moustache is not to be laughed at ... That window is free. Go about your business ... And thank your lucky stars that I'm in a hurry. Otherwise ... (*He goes to the other window.*)

TINY. What's he so happy about? Okay, so I talked about your moustache. It's not against the law to criticize moustaches, especially now that priests don't wear them anymore. (*At this moment the window closes in front of him. TINY is annoyed, but he has no choice but to get in line behind the GENTLEMAN with the moustache who looks at him suspiciously. A woman gets in line behind TINY. She looks a lot like one of Angela's friends. TINY looks at her and then says:)* Excuse me, but you're the spitting image of a friend of a friend of mine who makes her living as a ...

WOMAN. (*Annoyed, she looks at him coldly and interrupts.*) I beg your pardon?

TINY. Makes her living as a ... Oh ... I mistook you for one of my relatives who works for the Red Cross in Switzerland.

(Meanwhile another window opens. The WOMAN walks over to the window with her suitcase. The GENTLEMAN is talking a long time, but the WOMAN finishes her business quickly and seems ready to leave the window, so TINY picks up his things and prepares to move to the window she is vacating. But the WOMAN changes her mind and comes back to the window.)

WOMAN. I forgot ... could you make me a list of the forms I have to get from City Hall? Thank you... (*TINY is perplexed, as if losing a game of musical chairs. The other window becomes free, so TINY rushes over to it, but because he is in such a hurry he takes the WOMAN's suitcase with him by mistake*) Young man. Enough of your joking. That's my suitcase.

TINY. Excuse me ... I wasn't thinking.

WOMAN. That 's a fine excuse. First you confuse me with someone else, then you take my suitcase ...

TINY. Please don't think ... our suitcases really do look alike. And then ... you're so suspicious... Do you think I'm some kind of psychotic suitcase snatcher ... besides, it's cardboard. (*Goes to the window.*) Could you please ... (*But with a loud crash a barrier falls down closing the window.*) It's all your fault. Why didn't I leave you at home. (*He kicks the woman's suitcase.*)

WOMAN. What!! Are you insane?

TINY. Oh, I'm sorry. I thought it was mine ...

WOMAN. Sorry. Sorry. You should thank heaven that I'm not a man.

TINY. Thank you heaven. (*He makes a gesture to clean off the suitcase where he kicked it,and then moves to another window which shuts in his face.*) It's like going to confession at the automat. (*The woman leaves in a huff. TINY turns and trips over his own suitcase. He is about to punish the offending suitcase by kicking it, but stops himself with leg in midair. A waiter enters with a tray, cups and a coffee pot. He also looks like one of the friends.*) Jules! ...

WAITER. My name is Harry, not Jules ... in any case, if you want to order something you have to go to the bar. I serve only the clerks. (*He taps a spoon against a cup. As if by magic the sound of the spoon results in the immediate opening of the first window. The WAITER holds out a cup. The clerk takes it and smashes the window down again as TINY approaches holding out a form.)*

TINY. If I may, I'd like ... (*Meanwhile the WAITER has moved to another window. He taps the cup, it opens, and TINY rushes over.*) Excuse me, if I may ... (*Same result. TINY decides to get smart. He ignores the third window and moves to the fourth in anticipation of the WAITER's arrival, ready to thrust his document at the clerk as soon as he appears. The cup sounds and a window opens, but it is the fifth window. TINY rushes over to it, but he is too late. The clerk has already taken his coffee and disappeared.*) Doesn't this one drink coffee? (*Pointing to the fourth window.*)

WAITER. No. He takes tea with lemon. (*Takes a larger cup and places it in front of the fourth window which opens just long enough for the clerk to grab his tea before slamming shut.*)

TINY. That's it. I leave my friends because they make too much fun of me, and here I find their doubles mocking me even more. (*He kicks the suitcase in a rage. He shouts and jumps around in pain. Meanwhile the waiter swiftly takes back the empty cups from each of the clerks, the windows opening and closing like an assembly line. TINY arrives at each one too late, and gets his finger caught as the last one bangs shut.*) Ahi! My finger!!

WAITER. (*Snickering.*) Ha. Ha. He smashed his finger. Ha. He has a smashed finger...(*The WAITER laughs so hard he doesn't notice the arrival of the GENTLEMAN from earlier in the scene. They bump into each other and the cups fall on the ground. The windows open and the clerks laugh in unison. The windows shut. The WAITER, with the help of the GENTLEMAN, picks up the cups, then tries to clean the man's stained jacket. They keep apologizing to one another. The WAITER gets carried away with the cleaning, and begins polishing the man's nails as if he were giving him a manicure.*) Excuse me, I didn't see you ...

GENTLEMAN. No, it was my fault. I was looking at my documents ... I've made a mess for you.

WAITER. No, it's nothing. But your jacket ... look at the stains on the sleeves.

GENTLEMAN. A little water will wash it away ...

WAITER. Let's hope so... (*He spits on the jacket and tries to clean it off with his own sleeve.*) I'm so sorry.

(*He starts to walk away but TINY intentionally trips him with the suitcase. This time the WAITER's fall is catastrophic. Broken dishes everywhere. Loud crashing sounds. The GENTLEMAN goes to help the WAITER but TINY slides a package under his feet and*

*trips him too. The clerks open their windows
and stick their heads out to get a better view of
the fall. They laugh. TINY closes the
windows in a way that traps each of their
heads on the counter. Then he kicks the
WAITER, who has just finished picking up
everything. The kick sends the WAITER
flying out the door, and the GENTLEMAN
runs out, fearing that TINY will kick him too.
All the clerks shout for help.)*

TINY. Enough! Silence! ... I said that's
enough! Silence! Enough! Shut up! (*Locks the door
with a key.*) Now that I finally have the honor of
your full attention ... listen to me!!!! I've come
here on very important business: my pension. I
brought everything with me ... (*Opens the
suitcase. Takes out a large packet of documents,
and deposits a pile under each one of the clerks'
heads.*) Birth certificates ... residence papers ...
discharge papers ... unlimited liability
insurance ... declaration of permanent disability
... authorization forms ... duplicates of the
authorization forms ... triplicates of the
authorization forms ... carbon copy originals of
the authorization forms. I don't understand any of
them, but I did my duty, now you do yours: verify
them, sign them, stamp them. Put on the seals, the
counter-seals, the stamps,and the counter-stamps
... All I want to do is to leave here with the proper
papers to get my pension. (*He grabs the rubber*

*stamps hanging from elastic cords around the
necks of each of the clerks, and attaches them to
their foreheads. Then he moves to the side of the
windows and grabs a lever which is attached to the
counter on which he has placed all his papers to be
stamped.*) I've got no time to lose ... And to make
my intentions clear, I brought a little something
with me from Africa, that I swear I'll set off if any
of you tries to get smart with me. Take a look: a
model 38 hand grenade. (*He takes a bomb out of
his suitcase and puts it on the doorman's table. He
begins shouting commands.*) Round rubber
stamps. (*Two clerks respond by lowering their
heads to stamp his papers.*) Square stamps. (*Two
other clerks obey.*) All stamps. Stamp. Stamp.
Stamp. Stamp, stamp, stamp. All stamps. (*The
clerks do not obey.*) All stamps. (*They still don't
obey.*) Damn. It's stuck. (*He pulls on the lever,
trying to force it down. When he succeeds the
counter begins to shake rhythmically, up and
down under the noses of the clerks, whose
foreheads, equipped with rubber stamps, bob up
and down in alternating rhythms as they stamp
the bouncing documents. It all gives the
impression of an extraordinary futuristic
machine.*) Stamp, stamp, stamp, stamp. (*As the
rhythm builds, the action transforms itself into a
steam engine that chugs along with a final "toot-
toot" as it grinds to a stop.*) Toot-toot ... ding, ding.
We made it. And now all we need is my
registration card which we'll find in my personal

file. (*One wall is covered with filing drawers. TINY pulls out the one that interests him.*) The A's are here. S's over there. This must be the T's. Here it is. (*Puts the drawer under the face of the first clerk.*) Go on, find the file for Mr. Weather. First name Sunny, Cloudy, Stormy and first one who laughs get a bomb up his nose. (*The clerk picks out the file with his teeth. TINY narrates the search as if he were a game show host.*) It's the wheel of fortune. Round and round the clerk's mouth goes, but where it stops, nobody knows. Can he do it. Yes, that's it. He's hit the jackpot. It's me. Weather, Sunny, date of birth, distinguishing features ... race: Labrador Retriever ... No?!! .. Yes, that's what it says ... race: Labrador Retriever ... profession: hunter of birds: stunted tail: floppy ears, small teeth, apparently a mongrel ... Ha Ha. (*Laughs hysterically.*) Apparently a mongrel?! (*The clerks laugh. TINY grabs the bomb and removes the safety pin. The clerks stop laughing.*) Whose idea was it to play this stinking trick on me? Come on, who was it? I warned you not to make fun of me. Not to play around. I don't even let my friends make a fool of me anymore, and they used to pay me for it. ... A labrador retriever, eh? (*Lifts up his arm to throw the bomb.*) This will teach you. Go on, laugh. Laugh for the last time. Laugh. Ha, ha ha. (*The clerks would like to shout for help, but are struck mute with terror. TINY spins around, playing with the bomb as if it were on a wheel of fortune.*)

Place your bets, folks. Round and round the little bomb goes and where it lands, nobody knows ... ha ... ha ...ha

(*Sounds of banging and knocking at the door.*)

VOICE. Open up. What's going on ... Open up!

TINY. Look at their faces ... ha ... ha ... ha...

(*Blackout. During the blackout there are shouts and sounds of the door being broken down.*)

VOICES. Stop him. – Wait he has a bomb. – Grab it.

TINY. Step right up. Grab it if you can. First prize is a shiny medal. A little monkey for the gentleman. A balloon on string. (*Laughs like a madman.*)

(*The lights come up. TINY is handcuffed to a chair. Sitting in front of him is a police inspector. A plain clothes detective stands nearby.*)

TINY. (*Looking them over.*) A balloon with a string. (*He seems to recognize them.*) Get a load of that. Two more doubles. (*Turns to the inspector.*) Excuse me, but you wouldn't happen to have a twin brother ... an orthodox priest who runs a pastry shop on the side.

INSPECTOR. A priest in a pastry shop?

TINY. (*All in one breath.*) Yeah ... well, he's not really orthodox ... he just pretends to be an orthodox priest ... anyway he married me ... not in the sense that I married a priest ... not in the biblical sense ... but the fact is you look a lot like the man who owns the pastry shop ... so much so that I said to myself right away: he's the spitting image of the man in the pastry shop! (*As he speaks TINY moves his handcuffed arms in a way that suggests the unwinding of a skein of wool.*)

INSPECTOR. Enough of that, for heaven's sake. Listen, it's useless to keep ranting on like this. (*Without realizing it the INSPECTOR has got caught up in the game and moves his hands as if he were winding up the wool into a ball of yarn.*) Trying to pass yourself off as a madman is the oldest trick in the book, and it's not going to fool me. (*He realizes the absurdity of the game and throws away the imaginary ball of yarn. The detective catches it and puts it in his pocket.*) Come on. Be good. What's your name?

TINY. What's yours?

INSPECTOR. What do you mean, "What's yours?" I'm the one asking the questions around here.

TINY. Only you? No. That's not fair. Come on. Maybe your friend has a question too. Give somebody else a chance. Be a sport. Let's play for it. Okay. (*Moves his arms as if playing a child's game.*) One potato, two potato ... tell me when to stop ... three potato, four ...

INSPECTOR. Stop!

TINY. Okay. Stop on four potato. Good. (*Starts the count again.*) Four potato, five potato, six potato, seven ... Your turn ... (*Points to the INSPECTOR.*) He's not playing (*Points to the detective who slaps him. TINY blocks the slap with the palm of his hand. Another slap. Another block. There is a mechanical progression, and they end up playing a game of patty cake that finishes with the detective getting a big slap.*)

DETECTIVE. Stop clowning around, and answer the inspector's questions.

TINY. Oh, he's an inspector. Why didn't you tell me sooner. I was wondering why a priest with a pastry shop would want to put me in handcuffs ... Well, inspector, you know what I think. I think you're a hell of a nice guy.

DETECTIVE. (*Losing his patience, gives him a backhanded slap on the neck.*) Don't try to get personal.

TINY. Well he's getting pretty personal with me. Is there some article in the penal code that says an inspector's allowed to get personal with a citizen, but the citizen can't reciprocate.

DETECTIVE.Insolent dog. Who do you think you are? (*Slaps him in the face.*)

TINY. That's it. This brutality is getting out of hand. I'm leaving. (*Moves as if to leave.*)

INSPECTOR. (*Holding him down.*) Calm down. Come over here and sit down. And I'll try to address you more politely, okay?

TINY. You know Inspector, I've thought it over, and I think we might as well get personal. It's more intimate. And we were just beginning to break the ice.

INSPECTOR. You're beginning to break my balls! ... (*Gets control of himself after a sign from the detective.*) Okay. Name. Last name first.

TINY. Weather, Sunny, Cloudy, Stormy.

DETECTIVE.(*Losing his composure.*) Stop screwing around. The inspector may be a patient man, but I'm not. (*Slaps him with the back of his hand.*)

TINY. Come on, this is like beating up a slave with his hands tied. It's not fair. (*He sees another slap coming and ducks.*)

INSPECTOR. Why you ... (*The slap hits the inspector.*) That will be enough, detective. (*Turns back to TINY gritting his teeth.*) How much longer do I have to wait?

TINY. Just tell your slaphappy assistant to control himself and we can get on with it ... Now Sunny, Cloudy, Stormy Weather really is my name. And if you don't believe me, just look at these papers. That one for instance. (*Points to a paper sticking out of his suitcase.*) You'll see ...

DETECTIVE.(*Takes the paper and reads it.*) Ynnus Rehtaew.

TINY. Its' upside down.

DETECTIVE. Of course. (*Turns paper over.*) Sunny Weather. That's what it says. (*Gives the document to the Inspector.*)

TINY. Cloudy and Stormy are my middle names. I told you ...

INSPECTOR. (*Reading the rest of the paper.*) Veteran's Administration, Declaration of Permanent Disability ... What's this? Are you disabled?

TINY. Certainly: Second degree. (*To the detective who has gone white.*) I don't know where it was that I read about the severe penalties for the use of violence against the disabled ... especially when they are in a position from which it is impossible to defend themselves. Sergeant, you're in big trouble this time. (*Slaps him.*)

INSPECTOR. Unlock the cuffs, Sergeant.

(*The detective removes the handcuffs.*)

TINY. Isn't life funny. A person works his whole life to build up a career, and one day, a silly little thing knocks it all to pieces. All because of the bad habit of slapping people around. Bad hands. Shame on them. (*Slaps the hands of the detective, who wants to retaliate, but TINY stops him.*) No ... no. Disabled vet, remember. You know the saying, "Don't touch the disabled, even with a flower." Do you want some advice. Put those handcuffs on yourself.

(*Mechanically the detective starts to obey, but stops himself.*)

INSPECTOR. All right, can we continue? Sergeant, take notes, please. (*The detective takes out a notebook.*) From the top. First name: Sunny. Last name: Weather. Got it? (*The mortified detective nods his head "yes."*) Profession?

TINY. Hunting dog; race: Labrador ...

INSPECTOR. (*Distracted.*) Hunting dog ... (*He stands up suddenly.*) Now you're going too far. (*Losing control, he gets close to TINY.*) No punk like you is going to make fun of me like that.

TINY. Be careful, Inspector ... disabled veteran. Think of your family.

INSPECTOR. All right. (*He sits down again.*) But I warn you. Disabled veteran, or not, you better stop fooling around ... Now let's get to the bottom of this ... (*Pulls the bomb out of his pocket.*) Where did you get this bomb?

TINY. That's not a real bomb. It's only a shell. Allow me. (*He takes it in his hand, unscrews it, and pretends to throw it at the detective.*) Hey, Sergeant, you're dead.

(*The detective jumps backwards and ends up sitting on the inspector's lap.*)

INSPECTOR & DETECTIVE. (*With their arms raised.*) Stop joking around.

TINY. I'm not joking. I want you two to read what it says on this card ... out loud. (*He hands them the registration card.*) Two part harmony. Let's go. (*Threatens them with the bomb.*)

INSPECTOR & DETECTIVE. (*In unison with one sitting on the other and their four arms moving synchronously like hindu dancers.*) Sunny Weather, born March 24, 1954 in Sangiano, race: Labrador retriever ...

TINY. With a stunted tail, apparently a mongrel!

INSPECTOR. Unbelievable!

TINY. Yes, it's unbelievable. And you wanted to smash my face in because you thought I was making fun of you ... What am I supposed to do when I come here to collect my pension and discover instead that I have to pay a dog tax, wear a muzzle, and walk around on a leash. Can you blame me for wanting to throw a few hand grenades? (*Makes a gesture as if about to throw the bomb.*)

INSPECTOR. Okay. Okay. We'll straighten out this ugly joke as soon as possible; but now calm down and put that thing away.

TINY. Don't worry, there's no danger ... it's a cigarette lighter ... (*He opens it, flips a switch, make a flame, and lights a cigarette on it.*) You see, this is a joke too. ... I'm playing a joke on you

... (*He throws the strange lighter to them while it is still lit.*)

(*The inspector and detective are barely able to catch it.*)

INSPECTOR & DETECTIVE. No. (*Throwing it back to him.*)

TINY. (*Catching it on the fly.*) ... And you're playing a joke on me ... That way the whole world becomes a joke. But don't worry ... I'm used to it. It doesn't bother me.

INSPECTOR. Well, it bothers me. I can't stand jokes (*They continue the pantomime of synchronized gestures, building to a frenzy.*) Especially when they're perpetrated by public officials who have been entrusted with the protection of our citizens' rights and welfare. (*Turns to the detective who is still in his lap.*) Sergeant, I know you're very attached to your superiors, but I must ask you to get up.

DETECTIVE. Yes, of course. (*He gets up.*)

INSPECTOR. (*Still to the detective.*) I want to talk to all the clerks in this office ... Get to it. They'll find out what happens to people who joke around with serious business.

(*The detective opens the door and all the clerks who were listening at the keyhole fall into the room.*)

DETECTIVE. So you were listening through the keyhole?

INSPECTOR. Good. Now I won't have to waste time explaining things. Make yourselves comfortable. (*The clerks line up in front of him.*) What kind of farce is this? (*He waves TINY's papers under their noses, pacing back and forth like a drill sergeant.*)

TINY. (*Marching behind the inspector with evident satisfaction.*) Yeah, what is this?

INSPECTOR. Nobody knows anything about it, right? All right then, I'll tell you what it is. It's a bad joke. It's an insult to our citizens.

TINY. (*Prompting him.*) Who pay the taxes.

INSPECTOR. Who pay the taxes. ...

TINY. That pay your salaries ...

INSPECTOR. That pay your ... hey, let's take it easy.

TINY. Yes, yes, we'll take it easy, but you'll see. We'll get the answer.

INSPECTOR. I want to know who's responsible for this deplorable act which dishonors not only your department, but public servants everywhere.

TINY. (*Still prompting.*) Including me.

INSPECTOR.   ... including me ... and in defense of the honor and the dignity of ... of ...

TINY. the above mentioned.

INSPECTOR. Of the above mentioned ... thank you ... that I demand to know which one of you is guilty. I'll give you three minutes. Then ...

TINY. I'll put you all up against the wall.

INSPECTOR. I'll put you all up against the wall.

(*TINY performs a firing squad pantomime, miming that the machine gun is jammed. He takes it apart and puts it back together as a violin. He play a brief "Fugue" on the transformed machine gun.*)

TINY. Maybe shooting all of you would be a bit excessive. Maybe just a few: one, two, three. (*He starts to count the clerks.*)

FIRST CLERK. (*Taking a step forward.*) Can I speak?

TINY. No.

INSPECTOR. (*Stupified.*) No.

DETECTIVE. (*Parroting.*) No.

INSPECTOR. You have one minute left.

DETECTIVE. One minute.

FIRST CLERK. On behalf of my colleagues, I think I can give you an explanation.

TINY. See that, Inspector? Mass murder gets results ... Take this down Sergeant.

FIRST CLERK. The whole thing began fifteen years ago.

SECOND CLERK. We were still in the Vietnam War.

FIRST CLERK. One of the older workers here was forced into early retirement.

THIRD CLERK. A few months before he would have been entitled to a promotion.

(*Each CLERK takes a few steps forward before speaking and steps back into line afterwards.*)

TINY. Another good joke to add to my collection.

FIRST CLERK. As I was saying, the clerk, on whom fate had played this miserable trick ...

TINY. I didn't know you called your supervisors Fate. Commissioner Fate. Undersecretary of Fate. Assistant Department Manager Fate ...

INSPECTOR. Please let him finish.

TINY. I'm sorry. So what did he do, this victim of fate?

FIRST CLERK. He almost went insane ...

FOURTH CLERK. And as a desperate act of revenge against the injustice he had suffered, the clerk began making random changes in the registration files ...

SECOND CLERK. Since he had been in charge of those files for thirty years, he knew just what to do to create total chaos.

THIRD CLERK. For example, he re-arranged things so that we had a priest married to a forest ranger.

FIRST CLERK. One man died before he was born.

FIFTH CLERK. And there was a general who had never spent a day in the military

SECOND CLERK. Another was resurrected twenty years after his death, went to Argentina for a sex change operation, and married ...

THIRD CLERK. ... a mulatto from Martinique. (*The back and forth movements of the CLERKS begins to look like a traditional folk dance, with spins and changes.*) But all those changes were directed against the families of the people he blamed for his predicament.

TINY. (*Interrupting.*) Okay, but what do I have to do with it? What did I do to deserve being transformed into a dog ... a mutt!

FIRST CLERK. Do you have any relatives who worked in the department?

TINY. No.

FIRST CLERK. Maybe there was some one with a similar name?

TINY. A similar name? Not many people have a father as crazy as mine.

SECOND CLERK. I guess he just let things get out of hand.

TINY. (*Almost hysterical.*) Out of hand?!! I'll teach him to get out of hand with me. I'll put him out of hand, out of arm, and out of feet! I'll tear him to pieces!!! (*He grabs one of the CLERKS by the collar.*) Where is he? I'll give him a promotion ... to the moon. Where does he live?

SECOND CLERK. In the cemetery.

TINY. He's dead?

THIRD CLERK. Yes. About two months later. They say he did nothing but laugh ... and that his laughter was so contagious that his friends and relatives couldn't stop themselves from giggling at his death bed ... they were still laughing at the funeral.

FIRST CLERK. I was there. It was the funniest funeral I've ever been to.

ALL CLERKS. (*In chorus.*) What a load of laughs.

TINY. Come on, let's forget about happy funerals and get back to our story. How did you dig yourselves out of this mountain of falsification?

(*The CLERKS begin to move in all directions. TINY sits down to watch the show.*)

FIRST CLERK. At first everyone was desperate. Especially our superiors: the alterations were executed with such perfection, that it was impossible to restore order without personally contacting every individual concerned.

SECOND CLERK. Not to mention the dead ones.

THIRD CLERK. Or the ones who hadn't been born yet.

FIRST CLERK. There would have been a scandal ... an investigation, and inevitably a special prosecutor. (*The CLERKS move more and more frantically. The SERGEANT puts on white gloves to direct traffic.*) Not to mention a trial, and all the embarrassment it would cause for everyone involved, including some high placed government officials.

(*The INSPECTOR gets caught up in the game, but crosses the stage just as the SERGEANT/TRAFFIC COP was signalling stop. The SERGEANT repeatedly blows his whistle at the INSPECTOR, and is about to give him a ticket for jaywalking when the INSPECTOR pulls out his badge, and sticks it in the SERGEANT's face.*)

DETECTIVE. (*Stopping.*) Enough said ... (*Turns to the others.*) Move along. Move along. (*Then to the THIRD CLERK.*) You, keep going.

THIRD CLERK. We were saved by chance when a wing of the building was destroyed by fire. We collected all the incriminating documents and shredded them, blaming the loss on the fire.

THE CLERKS. (*In Chorus.*) Hallelujah!

TINY. All the documents, except mine.

THIRD CLERK. Yes, all but yours. I don't understand how we missed it.

TINY. (*Gets slowly to his feet, looks them all over, and begins aggressively.*) So you don't understand, huh? I'll tell you why? Because the name on the card wasn't one of yours ... so none of you gave a damn ... Last time you were saved

by a fire, but this time the fire's going to burn your
asses till they're cooked. (*To the INSPECTOR
and the SERGEANT.*) Not yours of course.
Nothing's going to save you ... I'm going to put
each one of you in a filing drawer and roast you
alive ... with an apple in your mouth. (*To the
INSPECTOR and the SERGEANT.*) We'll think
of something for you later. Now I understand why
your colleague included me in his revenge. I was
the back up fuse, the emergency reserve plan, in
case the first one fizzled out. Ha. Ha. (*He laughs
and turns to someone in the audience, as if he has
found the dead CLERK resurrected.*) Insane? No,
you were shrewd ... Ha.Ha. You had a wild card
up your sleeve. A joker. You were right to laugh
with your dying breath ... Ha. Ha. Listen, he's
still laughing. What a ...

   DETECTIVE. (*Seriously worried.*) He's
really losing his mind.

   INSPECTOR. Calm down. Don't get excited.
It's bad for you health. Everything is going to be
all right, you'll see. But first you have to sit down
and relax.

(*Everyone runs to get chairs to TINY and the
   INSPECTOR, who ends up sitting on nothing,
   falls to the ground with a thud.*

   TINY. That's easy for him to say.
   INSPECTOR. (*Paternalistically.*) Now let's
get this straight. You came here to speed up your

pension payments. But how many months, days, years will it take to clear all this up. Don't forget, you'll have to wait till the investigation is over before you can retrieve your true identity. The first step is to correct your registration status. For the rest, just relax, and I assure you that those who are responsible will not go unpunished. (*Turns to the CLERKS.*) And since you are the ones responsible for this mess, it would be in your own interest to give this case top priority. Is that clear?

FIRST CLERK. As far as the registration is concerned, there might be a solution, but it all depends on the gentlemen's willingness to collaborate ...

INSPECTOR. (*Turning again to the CLERKS.*) Hold on! I'm trying to meet you half way on this, but I can only go so far. I don't want to hear about the details, but if everything's not straightened out in three days, I'm going to write out arrest warrants for everybody in the department. And I'll make sure you spend the investigation period in jail. Get it? Goodbye.

DETECTIVE. (*To the INSPECTOR as he leaves.*) So long, chief.

INSPECTOR. See you later, pal. (*Leaves and comes back immediately walking backwards as if in a movie being run backwards.*) Get it? Goodbye. (*Signals the DETECTIVE.*)

DETECTIVE. Oh, yeah ... (*Lines up behind the INSPECTOR. They leave with synchronous steps, whose rhythms are dictated by the SERGEANT blowing his whistle.)*

TINY. All right, let's hear it. What's the plan?

CLERKS. Excuse us? *(They huddle together like a team of football players.)*

FIRST CLERK. *(Coming out of the huddle.)* If you would be kind enough to remain a labrador retriever for just a few more days, then ...

TINY. *(Threateningly.)* Then?

SECOND CLERK. *(Hesitantly.)* Everything would be resolved: it would only take three days. *(He consults with his colleagues in a whisper. They agree.)* Naturally we'd need your help.

TINY. *(Ironic, unconvinced.)* All right. What do I have to do?

FIRST CLERK. *(All in one breath.)* Turn yourself in, without a license or a muzzle, to the city dogcatcher.

TINY. *(Almost shouting.)* What?

THIRD CLERK. *(Moving backwards, ready to run.)* Naturally, the dogcatcher would be informed about our plan. The director of the pound is one of our former colleagues, and he wouldn't deny us a small favor.

TINY. *(Calm, chewing each word.)* In other words, you want me to pass myself off as a lost pooch. And then what happens?

FIRST CLERK. *(Only slightly reassured.)* You know, under the law, after three days in the pound, if no one comes to claim them, stray dogs are put to sleep in a gas chamber.

TINY. (*Distracted.*) Yes, I know that stray dogs ... (*Suddenly shouting like before.*) What? A gas chamber? I don't know if I like this plan; I'll have to think it over.

FOURTH CLERK. (*With a smile.*) No, you've misunderstood. We weren't planning to send you to the gas chamber. (*As if he were recounting the most obvious story in the world.*) After three days, the records will show that you are dead, as a dog. Then, once that problem is eliminated, you can present yourself to us with two witnesses to get back your real identity.

THIRD CLERK. (*In the same tone.*) Then, on the same day, you'll be able to collect the back payments on your pension, which I've roughly calculated to amount to something like ... (*All the clerks lift up their hands with their fingers spread. Tiny is obliged to do the same. The CLERK finishes his calculations by pulling on their fingers as if he were operating an adding machine.*) ... If you don't mind ... Ten thousand dollars.

TINY. (*Enthusiastically.*) Ten thousand dollars. That's a great price for a used coccyx. Dog catcher, here I come. I'd rather spend three days as a poor dog, than a hundred as a poor man. Long live bureaucracy!!!

(*All the CLERKS come downstage to sing the song of the bureaucrats. The fence curtain is drawn behind them so that the scenery can be changed.*)

CLERKS. WHO WAS THE GREAT BUREAUCRAT WHO INVENTED FORMS IN TRIPLICATE
TRANSIT PAPERS, AND VERIFICATION STAMPS
UNPERMISSABLE PRACTICES, AND ADDITIONAL TAXATION
INVALIDATED SIGNATURES, CERTIFICATES OF DISCHARGE
HONORARY DISCHARGES, OBLIGATORY GRATUITIES COMMON PROTOCOL, CERTIFIED BONDS?
NO STONE RECORDS HIS DATE OF BIRTH
PERHAPS HIS FILE'S LABELLED "ANONYMOUS" "ANONYMOUS"

BLACKOUT

ACT II

Scene 2

Lights up. Fence/curtain opens. We are in the city dog pound. There are several cages. The one in the center has a sign that reads, "Beware of the Man." TINY is reluctantly dragged in by a dogcatcher. He has a muzzle on his face and a dog collar around his neck. The kennel guard opens the central cage and tries to push him in. One of the DOGCATCHERS drags him in by pulling forcefully on TINY's leash.

TINY. Hey, take it easy with that leash ... a little respect for your fellow man.

FIRST DOGCATCHER. Get moving then ... If all the mutts were like you, I'd be pushing up daisies. Come on, take off your clothes. (*Keeps trying to force TINY into the central cage.*)

TINY. (*Breaks free and shouts with a high pitched head voice.*) What!!?

SECOND DOGCATCHER. That's the rule.

GUARD and DOGCATCHERS. (*In unison, as if reciting a lesson.*) The captured animal must be stripped of all accessories being worn at the moment of capture: flea collar, leash, doggy blankets, etc.

TINY. (*Gesturing like an orchestra conductor signalling his musicians to finish.*) Okay. Okay. I get it. You've learned your lessons well. An "A" for effort. (*Nasty.*) But as far as accessories go, all I've got is this collar, leash and muzzle. And I'll give them to you with pleasure. (*Takes them off and throws them violently at the DOGCATCHERS.*) And stop trying to push me around. I only went along with this charade to help out your friends. So if you don't start behaving more politely, I'm going to blow the whistle on everyone and you'll all be looking for new jobs. You'll be out catching cats. Is that clear? (*Approaches the SECOND DOGCATCHER.*)

FIRST DOGCATCHER. It's clear. It's clear. But the regulations require ...

TINY. (*Enters the cage, but comes out immediately holding his nose.*) Speaking of regulations, that cage stinks. Is that a regulation smell? (*With air of a drill sergeant.*) Come on. Scrub brush. Soap. Hot water. Clean it out. Get moving ... Now.

(*Unthinkingly the two of them stand at attention. The first DOGCATCHER turns on his heels and leaves.*)

VOICE FROM THE LOUD SPEAKER. Attention please. In a few minutes the pound will be opened to visitors interested in adopting our animal guests. We ask the visitors to refrain from molesting or feeding the guests in their cages. Stay away from cages marked, "Dangerous specimen." And remember that the gas chamber, especially during operating hours, is reserved for the exclusive use of our resident guests.

(*TINY listens with interest. Meanwhile the first guard, having returned with a brush and a bucket of water, begins to clean up. The visitors begin appearing. TINY browses around the cages, and stops in front of one of the cages, removing the sign from its bars. A woman stops in front of the cage to the right.*)

WOMAN. (*As if speaking about a baby.*) Pretty, pretty, pretty. Oh what pretty pointer.

TINY. (*Coming up behind her.*) That's not a pointer. It's a retriever.

WOMAN. (*Without turning around.*) How can you be so sure.

TINY. Because I'm a retriever too.

(*The WOMAN turns with an amused smile, but when she see TINY, who has put on his muzzle again, she screams and runs away.*)

FIRST DOGCATCHER. (*Running up to TINY.*) What are you doing? You can't go around scaring the visitors like that. The director will have my head. (*Grabs him by the collar.*) Come on. Your cage is clean now.

TINY. (*Entertaining himself by making puppy sounds.*) Okay. But leave me alone so I can get a little reading done. (*Pulls a newspaper out of his pocket.*) Would you mind shutting the door? Thank you. And please tell the doorman that I don't wish to be disturbed. You're very kind.

(*TINY opens the newspaper in front of his face while one of the keepers puts a sign on the bars of his cage. A strange gentleman in old fashioned clothes and a bowler hat, approaches the cage, grabs the sign and gets up on his toes in an effort to see what's behind the newspaper. TINY barks. Looks out over the newspaper, then disappears again. Annoyed by the man's insistent curiosity, he jumps aggressively towards the bars, barking and growling like a mad dog.*)

MAN. (*Jumps back, speechless at first. Then he very politely turns to the FIRST DOGCATCHER who is still there with the cleaning equipment.*) Excuse me. Are you sure that's a retriever?

FIRST DOGCATCHER. (*Mocking him openly.*) I don't know. They pay me to catch them, not to identify their breeds. But if the sign says so, then it's a retriever.

MAN. (*Convinced, without irony.*) Good. Then, I'll take him.

FIRST DOGCATCHER. (*Convinced the man is making fun of him.*) What?

MAN. (*Still serious. Holding out some bills.*) Here's the money for the license and the fine ... and here are my identification papers. I'd like to take him with me now.

FIRST DOGCATCHER. Are you joking?

MAN. (*Hurt. He has the air of a lucid madman.*) I don't see how you could suspect me of such a thing. Am I or am I not within my rights to take home the dog of my choice? This is the animal that interests me. I demand that you turn him over to me ...

TINY. (*Listening with great interest. Suddenly sticks his arm out of the cage and grabs the MAN with the bowler by the collar.*) Listen, you second hand Victorian relic ... (*Alluding to the man's nineteenth century clothing.*) If I hear you expressing any more "interest" in this "animal" that happens to be me, you're going to get a kick in the head that'll send you into emergency surgery.

MAN. (*Amazed, turning to the keeper.*) Excuse me, was that him talking or are you a ventriloquist.

SECOND DOGCATCHER. (*Just arrived.*) I'll explain everything, sir. (*Then whispers aside to the other two.*) Quiet, I know this one. He's crazy. (*Kindly taking the man's arm and leading him*

away from the cage. He speaks softly and sadly.)
You see, it's a sad story. In all outward
appearances, I agree, he looks like a dog. But he is
actually a man ...

MAN. (*Turning his head to verify TINY's
identity.*) No?!!!!!!!!

SECOND DOGCATCHER. (*Sighing sadly.*)
Yes, a man. Poor thing. He's lost his mind.

MAN. (*Sad.*) You mean he's insane? What
happened?

SECOND DOGCATCHER. It's a pathetic
story. He had a dog who ran away and ended up in
that cage ... but by the time the man arrived to
retrieve him, the poor dog was dead.

MAN. (*With a lump in his throat.*) In the gas
chamber?

SECOND DOGCATCHER. (*After a short
pause.*) No, suicide. Maybe he thought his master
had abandoned him ... (*Sighs.*) and in a moment
of despair ... (*Mimes the cutting of a throat.*)

MAN. Suicide? How?

SECOND DOGCATCHER. (*Begins to mime a
pistol shot, but has second thoughts.*) With a piece
of broken glass. He slit his wrists. The wife of the
master died that way, and you know how dogs
pick things up.

MAN. (*Staring into space, remembering.*) I
know. My dog was alcoholic. (*He tips his hat and
turns back to the cage.*) Poor man. He's mad with
grief. But how did he end up in there?

SECOND DOGCATCHER. (*Taking him again by the arm. They walk downstage together.*) Every day, during visiting hours, he comes and asks us to let him into the cage where his dog had died. We don't have the heart to say no. He's in such pain. Poor beast.

MAN. (*Stops. Turns to look into space.*) I understand ... yes, I understand. I, too, grieved deeply when Lincoln died.

SECOND DOGCATCHER. You were an abolitionist?

MAN. No. I was an illusionist. A Republican, but an illusionist. The finale of my magic act was voodoo economics. And Lincoln was a black poodle. (*He happily traces the dog's figure in the air.*) And when the pom-poms on his ears flopped down under his chin, he was the spitting image of Honest Abe. (*Short pause. He looks directly at the DOGCATCHER.*) He was an intelligent beast, you know. He even learned how to perform slight of hand. (*Raises his voice to grand eloquent tones.*) Can you imagine the effect on the audience of a canine magician!

SECOND DOGCATCHER. (*Leading him on.*) Amazing. A canine magician.

MAN. (*Almost in tears.*) Yes, but he died a few days before his theatrical debut. (*Sighing, very sad.*) When he died, I thought I'd go mad.

SECOND DOGCATCHER. It shows. (*Trying to hold back his laughter.*)

MAN. (*Suspiciously.*) What did you say?

SECOND DOGCATCHER. I said "One never knows."

MAN. (*Toying with the sign on TINY's cage. Suddenly angry with the DOGCATCHER.*) And I almost fell for it. Why have you been telling me these lies?

SECOND DOGCATCHER. (*Taken aback.*) What lies?

MAN. Don't play dumb with me. The description on this card fits him to a T: Labrador retriever, stunted tail, floppy ears, unmarked coat, thick dark hair on his head, short teeth. There's no doubt about it. It's him.

TINY. (*Aggressive, slaps him on the top of his bowler hat. Grabs him around the neck and pulls him back against the bars.*) That does it. Yes, I am a Labrador retriever. And since I'm also a mongrel bastard mutt, you better got out of here before I bite off your ear. (*Loosening his hold.*) I warn you that I have rabies, distemper and fleas. And when I'm done with your ear, I'll skin you alive.

MAN. (*Terrorized, adjusting his damaged hat.*) Is it true what he says?

FIRST DOGCATCHER. (*Trying to keep from laughing in his face.*) Very true. Don't you see how he's beginning to foam at the mouth.

MAN. (*Hysterical.*) How irresponsible of you. What does he have to do before you label him "Dangerous" .... bite someone? (*Moves back and forth as TINY jumps up and down howling in his cage.*)

TINY. Uhuuuuuuuu. Uhuuuuuuuu. Grrrr ..... Uhuuuuuuuu!!!

(*As the mad magician leaves, another gentleman arrives running. He grabs the whip from one of the guardians and begins lashing TINY severely.*)

DIRECTOR. Good. Down, dog, down.

TINY. Ehi. Ahi. Uhuuuu. Uhuuuu. (*Wounded in the leg he hops in pain.*)

DIRECTOR. Down, dog. (*TINY sits down immediately. The man turns authoritatively to the DOGCATCHERS.*) What's the matter with you. Can't you keep this animal muzzled? What king of dog catchers are you?

FIRST DOGCATCHER. (*Trying to take the whip out of his hand.*) Today is the day of the madmen. Who are you?

DIRECTOR. I'm the director. (*Takes a step forward and puts his foot in the cleaning bucket.*)

SECOND DOGCATCHER. Stop playing games. I know the director. It's Dr. Campbell.

DIRECTOR. It was Dr. Campbell, but this morning he was transferred to another department. (*He frees himself from the bucket.*) And since I am the director now, I'm going to institute a few changes. So listen up, or I'll use this on you too. (*Another step forward lands him*

*in another bucket. While trying to get out of it, he
leans back against the central cage.*)

TINY. (*Grabs the whip quickly. Ties up the
Director's legs and immobilizes him.*) Listen,
boss, you've already got a strike against you
because you look just like a friend of mine that I
can't stand. So I'm warning you. If you ever try to
brand me again with the mark of Zorro, I'm going
to come out and pluck you like a daisy, till there's
nothing let of you but the little yellow lump in the
middle. (*He pushes him away with such force that
the Director turns pirouettes across the stage.*)

DIRECTOR. (*Staggering, dizzy.*) What's that
man doing in a cage?

FIRST DOGCATCHER. (*Supporting him.*)
Excuse me, but didn't the other director tell you
about the favor we were doing for the veterans'
registration office?

DIRECTOR. Oh, yes, he told me. (*Moves
towards TINY, but stops at a respectful distance.*)
In any case you'd better conduct yourself in a
manner befitting an animal of your breed. (*He
takes the bucket off his foot.*) A race noted for its
meek and quiet behavior. Otherwise I won't even
wait for the three days to pass. (*His voice is
transformed.*) I'll throw you into the gas chamber
and be rid of you right away. Is that understood?

TINY. (*His head caught in the bars, almost
shouting.*) Do I understand? Oh, daisy. What's
this about not waiting three days for the gas
chamber and getting rid of me right away? We

made a deal that you'd only pretend to put me to
sleep after three days. It's supposed to be a fake.
(*Turning to the two DOGCATCHERS.*) Let's not
joke around with gas.

DIRECTOR. (*Gesturing like the Director of a
military band.*) I didn't make any deals with
anybody. And I've never faked anything in my
life. I've always believed in serious respect for the
law. If three days go by and nobody picks you up,
we'll finish you off. In a county plagued by
favoritism and special interests, the least we can
do is keep corruption out of the dog pound. And
now get out of my way. I want to meet the rest of the
staff. (*He puts his foot in another bucket, and
marches   off,   followed   by   the   two
DOGCATCHERS.*)

TINY. (*Stunned. He shakes the cage. But it
doesn't open. Crying.*) Mama. Mama. Murder.
Murder. (*Shouts to the other cages.*) Spaniels,
terriers, mongrels, unite. Let's organize an
escape. I don't want to end up in a gas chamber.
It's not fair. Do I look like a man's best friend?
Wake up. Rebel ... Do something. (*He waits,
hoping that something will happen.*) Not even a
bark. You bastards. You know what I have to say
to you. You disgust me. Good riddance. Anyone
who lets themselves by muzzled, clipped, and
beaten without even a whimper of protest deserves
to end up in a gas chamber. It makes me happy.
Look how happy I am. (*Breaks down into sobs that*

sound like dog whimpers. Just then the illusionist reappears. TINY shouts.) I don't want to die.

MAN. (*Jumps from fright.*) Oh, you ugly beast. (*He leaves.*)

TINY. Wait, sir. Please listen ... (*Barks, speaks, barks. This has no effect on the MAN, so TINY begins meowing. The MAN returns to the cage.*) I'd like to tell you something ... (*The ILLUSIONIST watches him for a moment, then turns to leave. TINY meows again, and the ILLUSIONIST returns.*)

MAN. What's wrong?

TINY. (*Begging.*) Sir, get me out of here. Save me. They've trapped me ... they're really going to put me in the gas chamber ... they're all nasty, especially the daisy ... Please take me away ... be kind.

MAN. (*Moved, fatherly.*) My dear pooch, I'd love to take you home. I've been looking all my life for an animal like you to take the place of my poor Lincoln. But try to understand. How could I keep you in the house. You'll get over the fleas and distemper, but you can't fool around with rabies. If you bit me ...

TINY. (*Passionately begging.*) No, no. I don't have anything. I'm in perfect health. That was just a story I made up to try to be funny. (*Enter one of the DOGCATCHERS.*) Look, there's the guard. Ask him to tell you what's happened, and then, when you hear the truth, you'll take me away from here. And you won't be sorry. I'll be good. I'll do everything you tell me. I'll eat my dog food and biscuits. I'll fetch your paper, your slippers, your pipe. If you want I'll even pee against a tree. Just get me out of here. (*Barks and yelps.*)

(*All the other dogs join him.*)

MAN. (*Turning to the DOGCATCHER.*) Listen, about this retriever ... (*The dialog of the two men is lost in the barking of the dogs. It's feeding time. In fact, the DOGCATCHER distributes food to the cages as he talks, nodding in agreement as he moves from cage to cage. He takes the money, signs a card, and goes over to open TINY's cage. He puts a collar and muzzle on him. The ILLUSIONIST takes the leash.*) It's done. From this moment on, you are no longer a stray dog. You have a master. But I'm warning you that if you don't behave yourself like you promised, if you do anything nasty, I'm going to take you back to the pound. Okay?

TINY. Yes, yes, okay. But before we leave, will you let me be nasty one more time? Just a little?

MAN. Okay, as long as it's the last time.

TINY. Thank you. (*He grabs the whip from the hand of the DOGCATCHER, disappears to the right, and reappears a moment later chasing the DIRECTOR with the whip.*) Jump, boss, jump. Be strong. We have to eliminate favoritism and special interest. Every one should have a chance to be whipped. The law demands equal opportunity for all: dogs, men, cats and bosses too!! (*Like a circus animal trainer, TINY makes the three of them line up. Then with a crack of the whip, he makes them step forward, jumping as they were horses in the circus ring. They spin, pirouette, and gallop.*)

(*The routine is accompanied by a crescendo of circus music.*)

BLACKOUT

ACT II

Scene 3

As the lights go up the ILLUSIONIST rolls across stage in a wheelchair in front of the fence/curtain.

MAN. (*Shouting at full voice.*) Sunny. Sunny. Come here Sunny. Look how he ignores me and he promised to be faithful and obedient. He's going to give me another stroke ... That's what I get for taking the word of a dog ... a mongrel retriever. Who ever said that mongrels were the most affectionate, who? (*Raising his eyes to heaven.*) Lincoln. My Lincoln. You were a real dog. (*Makes a fist with is left hand and caresses it with his right hand as if it were a dog's head.*) You were the only one who really loved me. Ah, the way you wagged your tail for me ... this one never does. Not only is he tail-less, he doesn't even have a stump. And he's lazy besides. He never pays attention when I try to teach him the tricks of the trade. The few magic tricks I've taught him have cost me my health. A stroke put me in this wheelchair. And to think that I saved that mongrel's life. He wishes I were dead. I sent him out a half hour ago to get a newspaper, and he's still not back. Sunny. Sunny. (*The sounds of TINY barking are heard from outside.*) I told you a thousand times that I don't want you reading my newspaper. A dog that reads the newspaper! And on the street! Who knows what people will think! Come over here and present yourself properly.

TINY. (*Enters on all fours, still barking. Holds the paper between his teeth. Wears a scotch plaid blanket on his trunk and ragged wool long underwear on the rest of his body. He comes up to the ILLUSIONIST and gives him his newspaper.*) Here. Enjoy your newspaper.

MAN. And the bread and eggs and other things I asked you to buy ... Where are they?

TINY. Inside the newspaper.

MAN. (*Unfolding the newspaper.*) There's nothing in here.

TINY. Impossible I'm sure they're in there. I remember opening up the newspaper ...(*He takes the newspaper in his hand and holds it out in front of his master imitating the gestures of an ILLUSIONIST.)* ... and saying, "Could you please give me two eggs." And they gave me two eggs. *(Mimes the action.)* I took the two eggs and folded them up inside the newspaper. Are they there or not? Should we look and see?

MAN. *(Holding his breath.)* Yes.

TINY. *(Behind it.)* Op. There's the two eggs. Then I said "Could I have some bread." They gave me bread, and I put it under the newspaper. Should we see if there's any bread in there?

MAN. Yes.

TINY. Op. There's the bread. Then I said, "Listen, I'm tired of waiting around. Just give me the rest of the stuff without talking about it." They gave me everything else, and I put it all in the newspaper. Should we see if it's there? Op. There's the rest of it. *(He pulls out a tray overflowing with fruits, vegetables, salamis, and other produce. He rests the tray on the palm of his master's hand, and makes him lift up his other hand to imitate a grocer's scale. As he presses on one hand, the other lowers and raises.)* See. The exact weight. To the gram. You thought I was a failure, that I couldn't learn your tricks. Watch: One, two, three. Now you see it. Now you don't. *(Everything disappears.)*

MAN. *(With child-like enthusiasm.)* Wonderful. You deserve a treat. I'll give you ...

TINY. *(All in one breath.)* Give me back my trousers.

MAN. (*Shrewdly.*) Why? So you can run
away? No. No pants. But since you've learned
your lessons so well, I'm going to take you to see
an old friend of mine who runs a circus. Ha. Ha.
And when he sees you performing the tricks I've
taught you ... Ha. Ha. ... I can't wait to see his
face already. (*Imitating his voice.*) "What? A
canine magician? I never saw anything like it.
How much do you want for him?" (*Taking the
attitude of the king of clowns.*) "He's not for sale."
"Okay, then I'll rent him: a thousand dollars a
month." "No." "A week." "No." " A day." "Yes."
A thousand dollars a day, and zam, balooey.
Jackpot. (*Insanely pleased.*) And do you know
what I'm going to do with all that money?

TINY. Give it to a hospital for
underprivileged dogs?

MAN. (*Dismissing him with a cynical
chuckle.*) Let the dogs die. I never did like dogs,
anyway. I'm much more fond of cats. I'll use the
money to buy hundreds and hundreds of cats. Cats
of all colors, sizes, and breeds. Because I love
cats. (*He caresses the back of his left hand as if it
were a cat.*) Meow. Meow. Prrr. Prrr. Too bad
you're not a cat.

TINY. (*Playing the orphan.*) But I can be a
cat, really I can. Don't you remember how I
meowed at the pound? Meow ... purr. (*The meow
finishes with TINY spitting in the master's face.
Then he makes his hands into cat paws and claws
at the master.*) Pfuuuu. Pfuuuu.

MAN. What's got into you. You spit in my face.

TINY. (*Kicks the wheelchair and knocks it over.*) Sure I spit in your face, because you're a stinker and a madman. So it was all a lie. That you loved dogs. That you needed my protection.

MAN. (*Terrorized, cowardly.*) Don't be jealous. Come here and I'll tell you the truth. I only buy cats to sell them again at a profit. You have no idea how much money there is in cats ... When you think that half of the furs sold as leopard are actually dyed cat skins.

TINY. (*Meows and spits.*) Double stinker. Not only are you making a profit off of my skin, but off the cats' skin too. Damn you. Frrsptu...

MAN. (*Standing up off the wheelchair.*) Be a good puppy.

TINY. And you can walk too. You were just pretending to be a cripple to make me feel sorry for you. You were taking advantage of my tender heart to keep me from leaving you... Bastard. (*Kicks the wheelchair again.*)

MAN. (*Grabbing him by the collar.*) Down, dog, down. (*Forces TINY to his knees.*) I'll show you what happens to dogs who disobey their masters... I 'll chain you up and beat you to a pulp.

TINY. And I'll bite you. Take that. (*He bites him on the hand. The ILLUSIONIST screams and lets him go.*) And now I've got a surprise for you. I do have rabies.

MAN. No?!! (*Looks at his hand in shock.*)

TINY. Yes ... I've got the most poisonous form of rabies known to man or dog. Republican rabies. And now that I've attacked you, you've got them too. Goodbye.

MAN. (*Crying in desperation.*) No. Sunny. Sunny ...

TINY. Down, dog, down.

BLACKOUT

ACT II

Scene 4

A section of a first class railroad car. We see only a passenger compartment and a bathroom on the extreme right. As the curtain / fence opens, we see a gentleman in pajamas sleeping in the compartment. TINY, still in his long underwear, crawls down the corridor. He sees a folded pair of pants in the compartment, grabs them, and locks himself in the bathroom. The CONDUCTOR arrives and wakes up the gentleman delicately.

CONDUCTOR. Mr. Secretary, we'll be there in fifteen minutes... (*Shakes him.*) Mr. Secretary.

POLITICIAN. (*Stretching.*) Oh, my back is all cramped.

CONDUCTOR. Of course, the bed ... could have been better.

POLITICIAN. Yes, but the express train doesn't stop in this one-horse town. Why do they always send me out in the middle of nowhere. (*He rummages through his bag of toiletries.*)

CONDUCTOR. Excuse me ... (*He goes out to the corridor where he see TINY who is now wearing the POLITICIAN's pants, and who jumps back into the bathroom when he sees the CONDUCTOR coming. The CONDUCTOR becomes suspicious and knocks on the door.*) Sir, may I see your ticket please. Sir. Are you sick? Don't try any tricks with me. I'm warning you, if you don't come out right away, I'll open the door with my key. (*He takes a key out of his pocket, puts it in the lock, but TINY pulls on the handle, and a cracking noise is heard. The CONDUCTOR pulls out his key and looks at it.*) Dammit. It's broken. You're going to pay for this too if you don't get out of there now. (*Short pause.*) Okay. I'll wait. And at the next stop, I'll call the police.

(*TINY is inside with the doorknob in his hand. Meanwhile the POLITICIAN in the compartment is looking for his pants.*)

POLITICIAN. I'm sure I put them in this luggage rack. (*Leans his head out of the compartment.*) Conductor. My pants!

CONDUCTOR. What's wrong?

POLITICIAN. I can't find my pants. They're gone.

CONDUCTOR. (*Looking in the corridor.*) Impossible.

POLITICIAN. I remember putting them there. Someone must have stolen them while I was asleep. Fortunately, I put my wallet in the suitcase.

CONDUCTOR. Lucky for you.

POLITICIAN. Lucky my ass. How can I get off the train without my pants?

CONDUCTOR. Don't you have another pair in your suitcase?

POLITICIAN. Yes, I have two pair, but they're not dressy enough. I can't go to the inauguration in a tailcoat and scotch plaid trousers.

CONDUCTOR. That's a problem. But what can you do?

POLITICIAN. (*Looking at the CONDUCTOR's black pants.*) You can give me yours. They're not exactly elegant, but they're black, and they look like they're about my size.

CONDUCTOR. And I'm supposed to go around in my underwear?

POLITICIAN. No. You can have a pair of my pants. Pick the ones you like best, and try them on. Meanwhile I'll go to the bathroom.

CONDUCTOR. Well, okay.

POLITICIAN. Thank you. You're very kind. I'll remember you.

CONDUCTOR. Oh, thank you, Mr. Secretary. (*The politician goes out into the corridor and comes across TINY who has come out of the bathroom with the doorknob still in his hand. He doesn't know what to do with it, so he puts it in his pocket. TINY goes quickly past the compartment where the CONDUCTOR is standing with his pants off. He has taken the tools of his trade out of his pants pockets and is trying to open the politician's suitcase, but it won't open.*) Damn. It's locked. (*Goes cautiously out into the corridor, afraid of being seen in his underwear. He knocks on the door of the bathroom at the left, in which TINY is hiding.*) Mr. Secretary. ... He must be in that one, over there. The other character must have slipped away. (*He goes outside the door of the bathroom on the right, where the POLITICIAN is brushing his teeth.*) Mr. Secretary.

POLITICIAN. Who is it?

CONDUCTOR. The suitcase is locked. I didn't want to look through your jacket for the key without asking you first.

POLITICIAN. (*Gargling, distracted.*) No it's not in the jacket. It's in the back pocket of my pants ...

CONDUCTOR. In your pants?

POLITICIAN. (*Realizing what he's said as he gargles, and almost choking.*) Pffui ... It was in my pants. (*Coughs.*) No what? ... Wait, if you have a pocket knife, we can force open the lock. (*He tries to open the door to the bathroom.*)

CONDUCTOR. Yes, I've got a penknife. (*Takes one out of his jacket pocket.*)

(*TINY has returned to the POLITICIAN's compartment. He takes a dress shirt from the luggage net and puts it on. He also takes the jacket that is handing from the window. Only after he puts it on does he realize it's a tuxedo with very long tails. TINY grabs the tails with curiosity and flaps them as if they were wings, almost hoping to take off and fly.*)

POLITICIAN. There's no doorknob in here. Could you open it from out there with your key?

CONDUCTOR. I'd be happy to, but my key's broken.

POLITICIAN. Well, do something. I can't stay here locked in the toilet. When do we get into the station?

CONDUCTOR. We're almost there. (*Pulls all kinds of things out of his jacket pocket that might help him open the door.*) I don't know what to do.

POLITICIAN. Hurry. Call the other conductor. He'll have a key.

CONDUCTOR. He has one, but he's at the other end of the train, and to open the door to the next car I need the same key that's broken. We'll just have to wait till the next stop.

POLITICIAN. Not a chance. I have to get off at the next stop ... with my pants. Sound the alarm. Stop the train. You've got to get me out of here now!

CONDUCTOR. It's no use. The train's already stopping on it's own. Excuse me, but I have to go and put my pants back on.

POLITICIAN. No you don't. You gave me those pants, and I'm not going to let anybody take them away.

(*Meanwhile TINY has finished dressing himself. He's fixing his tie and putting on this top hat.*)

CONDUCTOR. But I can't do my job if I don't get off the train. And if I don't get off, how can I get the key from my colleague?

(*The train stops.*)

POLITICIAN. Shout out to him through the window.

(*TINY gets ready to leave. The STATIONMASTER appears. TINY gets off and finds himself between two policemen in formal dress. Resigned, he offers them his arms to be handcuffed. A gentleman with a three-colored scarf around his waist welcomes him. One of the policemen takes his suitcase, grabs the CONDUCTOR's pants,*)

*wraps them in a suitcase, and passes them to
the other policeman.)*

CONDUCTOR. (*Still pressed against the
bathroom door.*) But he won't be getting off the
train. It's not his station.

POLITICIAN. Then do what you want, but I
warn you, if you don't get me out of here in time,
I'll report you. I'll have you fired. I'll ruin you.

CONDUCTOR. (*Runs to the compartment and
finds it empty.*) My pants. Where are my pants?

(*The group has gone, accompanied by the sounds
of a fanfare. The STATIONMASTER looks
for the CONDUCTOR.*)

STATIONMASTER. Hey, Conductor. Where
are you?

CONDUCTOR. (*Leaning out.*) I'm in here.

STATIONMASTER. Well, aren't you getting
off? Who's going to signal for departure?

CONDUCTOR. I was just looking for my
pants ... They've disappeared, and I can't very
well go out looking like this. (*He shows himself
in his underwear.*)

STATIONMASTER. You've gone mad.

CONDUCTOR. I took them off for the Visiting
Secretary. He was insistent. He wanted them at
any cost.

STATIONMASTER. The Secretary wanted your pants. But which Secretary are you talking about?

CONDUCTOR. The one who's locked in the toilet.

STATIONMASTER. But the Visiting Secretary we were expecting has already left the train. Look, he's over there with the mayor and the other town officials.

CONDUCTOR. Then who have I got in there?

STATIONMASTER. Beats me. But I don't know why you'd take off your pants for him if he doesn't even work for the government.

CONDUCTOR. Now I know who it is ... It's the same character that locked himself in there before. That's why he's pretending he can't get out. He's passing himself off as the Secretary while the real Secretary left with my pants, thinking I'd already taken a pair of his. As soon as I get him out of there, I'll murder him. No. First I'll take his pants, then I'll murder him.

STATIONMASTER. Murder whoever you want, but let's get this train out of the station. We're already late. (*He raises his flag. We hear the noise of the locomotive building up steam, and we have the impression that the train is leaving the station, because the STATIONMASTER slides off sideways across the proscenium until he disappears into the wings.*)

SECRETARY. (*Shouting.*) Stop. Stop. Don't let the train leave. I have to get off. Conductor. Open the door!

CONDUCTOR. (*Taking off his jacket.*) Don't worry, I'll open it. I'll break the whole door down. Then I'll teach you to play tricks on people who work for a living. Your career in government is over, you fraud.

POLITICIAN. My career's over? What are you saying? Oh, no. Tell the congressional investigators I didn't know anything about the arms deal. I swear. I'm innocent. Trust me. Trust me.

BLACKOUT

(*Military band music plays as the set changes and continues as a backdrop for the next scene.*)

ACT II

Scene 5

The lights go up, and with the curtain / fence closed behind him, we see TINY in a tuxedo, flanked by the town officials and their wives. They raise their glasses in a toast.

ALL. Cheers.

MAYOR. (*He listens to one of the officials who's whispering in his ear. Then he turns to TINY with a wide malicious smile.*) Mr. Secretary, we have a wonderful surprise for you ... Your wife is here.

TINY. (*Spitting out the wine that was in his mouth.*) My wife? (*Coughs.*)

MAYOR. Ah. I knew you'd be pleased. An unexpected treat, isn't it?

TINY. Yes, it is unexpected. (*Continues coughing as he slaps the MAYOR on the back.*)

OFFICIAL. She told me you'd be surprised.

TINY. More than surprised. Surprised is not the word.

MAYOR. (*Friendly, man of the world.*) She arrived last night, but asked me to keep it a secret until the toast. Guess why?

TINY. Why? See how well I guessed. Why?

OFFICIAL. Because today is your wedding anniversary.

TINY. That's it. You guessed it.

OFFICIAL. She told us you'd probably forgotten.

TINY. (*Laughing stiffly.*) She told you, yes. Ha, ha, ha.

MAYOR. (*Moves towards the wings, and extends his arm as if the were introducing a singer.*) You can come out now. (*TINY closes his eyes and when he opens them he finds ANGELA standing in front of him.*) Mr. Minister, your wife.

TINY. (*Takes a step back.*) Angela.

ANGELA. (*Takes two steps forward.*) Sunny.

TINY and ANGELA. (*In unison.*) What are you doing here?

MAYOR. (*Paternal matchmaker.*) Come on. Don't stand there looking at her like that. She came all this way to celebrate your anniversary. That means she loves you, doesn't it? I'll leave you two alone, but only for five minutes, no more. They'll be waiting for us to lay down the first stone. (*He moves away and joins the other officials.*)

TINY. (*Holding his breath.*) Are you married to the Secretary?

ANGELA. (*Dismissing the idea.*) No, we're just friends. I needed to see him, so I passed myself off as his wife. Lucky he never arrived. Who know what kind of fuss he'd raise. He's so boring, and he's sexist besides. Do you believe he forces me to wear this dress backwards because is has a low neckline. Look. (*She turns around and shows him her back which is naked to the waist.*) Don't you think he's a sexist.

TINY. (*Teasing her, emphasizing "hard core."*) Yes, he's a hard core sexist.

ANGELA. (*Not following his game.*) It's a good thing he never showed up. (*As if seeing him now for the first time.*) Oh, Sunny. I'm so happy we found each other again. (*Notices the tuxedo.*)

Looks like you've moved up in the world. What kind of work are you doing?

TINY. Well, I started out as a dog.

ANGELA. (*Understanding.*) Yeah, it's always tough at the beginning. (*Returns to her tone of a few moments before.*) Oh, Sunny. I'm so happy we found each other again. I hope the Senator doesn't come and ruin everything.

TINY. (*Becoming sure of himself.*) Don't worry, he won't be coming.

(*Every so often a Waiter passes by to refill the glasses. TINY takes several refills.*)

ANGELA. How can you be so sure? Do you know him?

TINY. Of course I know him. How else would I be here?

ANGELA. He sent you to take his place?

TINY. No. He doesn't know anything about it.

ANGELA. He's in trouble, huh?

TINY. Well ... (*Laughs.*)

ANGELA. I knew he'd end up like this. He thought he was smarter than all the rest of them, but you'll see. They'll steal the pants off him.

TINY. They already did ... (*Laughs in a high voice, then suddenly becomes lucid and melancholy.*) But how did you get mixed up with him?

ANGELA. (*Turning away.*) Because of you.

TINY. (*Surprised, forcing her to look him in the face.*) Because of me?

ANGELA. Well, if you promise not to laugh, I'll tell you.

TINY. (*Reassuring.*) I won't laugh.

ANGELA. (*Speaks without pauses, without expression.*) When you left you said, "We'll see each other again," and I said it too. "We'll see each other again." (*The waiter comes back with a tray of glasses. TINY empties his, passes his glass to the girl, and takes another.*) But days and days went by and we didn't see each other again. And since I had such a strong desire to see you ... You're not laughing?

TINY. (*Moved.*) You wanted to see me?

ANGELA. (*Continuing in the same tone.*) Yes, I even went looking for you in some bars. Nobody knew where you were, so I went to Washington to look for you.

TINY. (*Short pause.*) To Washington, to look for me?

ANGELA. (*Looking away.*) To Washington. I went to all the government offices. I walked all over town. I saw so many people. (*Pause. She looks him in the eyes.*) But I didn't see you.

TINY. (*Punching the fence.*) Damn. If you'd only gone to the dog pound ... zac (*Makes a gesture that means "I was there."*)

ANGELA. The dog pound?

TINY. (*Quickly, making little of the story.*) Yes, the municipal dog pound, cage number twelve ... But it's a long story. Go on, so how did you meet the Senator.

ANGELA. I was just getting to that: So one day I met a man who was the spitting image of the orthodox priest ...

TINY. (*Happy, he stops her and continues the story in the same tone.*) ... who was actually a police inspector without his moustache.

ANGELA. (*In a hurry, spitting out her words.*) No. It was the Senator. I said, "How ya doin', priest?" He laughed. We joked about the coincidence, and we became friends.. (*Pause. Takes his hands.*) And it was a good thing we did, because now you and I have found each other again.

TINY. Speaking of coincidences, don't the people here look familiar?

ANGELA. Yes, they look a lot like the guys in your gang, and the women look a little bit like my friends.

TINY. (*Sighing with relief.*) I'm glad you think so too. I was beginning to think there was something wrong with me. For the longest time I've been seeing the same faces over and over again. The only one I didn't see was yours.

ANGELA. Me too. But I'm so happy to have found it again.

(*The waiter passes by again. TINY drinks another glass.*)

ANGELA. You look wonderful dressed as a Senator. It makes you seem even ... tinier.

TINY. I feel wonderful. (*Sways, already a little tipsy.*) I never felt so wonderful in my life.

ANGELA. I believe it. With the career you've made for yourself. I see you've even learned to walk without looking back over your shoulder. You remember?

TINY. I remember. I remember. The only thing I don't remember is what I'm supposed to be doing here.

MAYOR. (*Arriving at their side.*) Come now, Senator: the ground breaking ceremony for our new school.

TINY. Ah, yes. The school of hard rocks.

MAYOR. (*Laughs obsequiously.*) Your husband has such a great sense of humor. This way please.

(*The curtain/fence slides open revealing a construction site full of flags. Some pillars. Some poles. A red, white and blue ribbon held on each end by two gentlemen on opposite ends of the stage. TINY, staggering visibly, is taken to the front of the ribbon. Scissors are offered to him on a pillow. TINY grabs them with detachment and shows them to the spectators after having proven their effectiveness by snipping off part of a feather on the hat of a woman standing nearby. Then he grabs the ribbon, and cuts it without letting the parts fall. With elegant gestures he folds the cut ribbon into many tiny pieces and puts them into the top hat of one of the spectators. He passes his hand over the hat with a magician's gesture, and pulls out of the hat dozens of tiny American flags on tiny flagpoles, which he hands out to the spectators. They are amused and applaud.*)

MAYOR. *The MAYOR speaks through a microphone.*) And now ladies and gentlemen, and now before we begin the ground breaking ceremony for our new school, we would like the good Senator, who honors us with his presence, to present our teachers with outstanding achievement awards for everything they have done ... (*The microphone malfunctions and we only hear fragments of the speech as we watch the MAYOR's mouth move.*) ... justice ... liberty for all ... our great country ... the glory ...love ... America ...

(*Everyone applauds. Some medals are brought out on a pillow. TINY grabs one and pins it on the chest of the first gentleman who steps up to him. He embraces him and goes on to the next. He finds himself in front of a large-breasted woman. He is embarrassed and doesn't know where to pin the medal. Finally he decides. He turns her around and pins it onto her back, and then embraces her with even more embarrassment. The spectators applaud each award. When TINY gets to ANGELA, there are no more medals left on the pillow, so he approaches one of the previous prize winners and excusing himself with a smile, plucks off the medal, so that he can put in onto ANGELA and embrace her. He has another idea. He gestures for the pillow-bearer to approach. The pillow is empty, but with two fingers TINY squeezes the nose of the bearer and pulls out a medal as if by magic. He returns to ANGELA, pins it on her and embraces her. He looks at her happily. He want to embrace her again, but without another medal, he can't. He goes to the pillow-bearer and repeats everything: extracting the medal from his nose, pinning it on, the embrace. TINY returns to the bearer again, who this time stops him with a gesture, and pulls a medal out of his nose by himself. The bearer gives the medal to TINY who pins it on ANGELA. Everyone applauds.)*

MAYOR. (*The MAYOR approaches TINY and taps him on his shoulder. TINY pins a medal on him and embraces him.*) Thank you Senator, and now would you do us the honor of placing this parchment in the cornerstone of the school?

TINY. (*After embracing ANGELA still another time.*) The honor is all mine. (*He grabs the parchment, unrolls it, shows it to the audience, rolls it up again, puts it in the cornerstone, lights a match, puts in into the hole and sets off a lively display of fireworks. Explosions and lights everywhere. A mad fanfare of music. Everyone runs away in terror. TINY and ANGELA remain alone, continuing to embrace each other.)*

ANGELA. Oh, how beautiful ... it's really you.

OFFSTAGE VOICE. You can't run away from me ... I'll get you yet. (*The CONDUCTOR runs onstage, still in his underwear, followed by the SENATOR in his pajamas. They both disappear backstage.*)

ANGELA. (*Leaving TINY and following them.*) Hey, Senator, wait for me.

(*The CONDUCTOR runs on again, recognizes TINY, and chases him offstage.*)

ACT III

Scene 1

*Colonial styled bedroom, with a four poster canopy
bed if possible. Double doored entrance. One
door that goes to the bathroom. A sofa and two
armchairs on the right. On the left is a screen
with a small desk in front of it. The entrance
door opens. The MAYOR leads TINY into the
room, handing him the key.*

MAYOR. Please, make yourself comfortable.
Here's the key ... (*TINY puts it in his pocket.*)
How do you like it?

TINY. (*Looks around.*) Not bad. And you
were saying that George Washington slept in this
bed?

MAYOR. Yes, he did. Before it became a hotel,
this place was a colonial plantation.

TINY. It's extraordinary how many beds
Washington slept in. Same with Napoleon. If you
believe all the stories, you'd think they never had
time to do anything but sleep.

MAYOR. (*Openly admiring.*) Ha. Ha. I
never thought of that ... You know you're the
funniest Senator I ever met.

TINY. (*Pointedly, but without dwelling on the issue.*) Maybe that's because I 'm less of a Senator than you think ... (*He lets himself fall onto the couch which is on the right side of the room.*) Excuse me if I sit down, but after all that running ... I haven't run so much since I was a retriever ...

MAYOR. What?

TINY. (*Almost whispering.*) Nothing, nothing ... just reminiscing about the early days of my political career.

MAYOR. (*Full of adulation.*) I understand. In any case, excuse me for repeating myself, but you were magnificent today: the fireworks the magic tricks. A politician and an illusionist, all in one. I never could have imagined it.

TINY. (*Nonchalant.*) Well, nowadays, you never know what to expect from politicians: you've got acrobats, tight rope walkers, contortionists, jugglers, actors, ventriloquists and escape artists. The illusionists are the most common. They can do a little of everything.

MAYOR. Ha Ha. If they were only listening now.

TINY. (*Pointing to the three suitcases on the table.*) Whose are they? I only stole ... I mean brought, one.

MAYOR. They're your wife's. She slept here last night.

TINY. In Washington's bed? It's a good thing the Father of our country' s been out of action for a while, or I'd be jealous. Well, I hope she at least got rid of the guy in the pajamas.

MAYOR. Pardon me?

TINY. Uh, no, I was just saying that I lost track of Angela in the confusion and now I can't find my pajamas. (*Pretends to rummage through the suitcase he left on the bed.*)

MAYOR. Don't worry, I'll give you a pair of mine. My room's just down the hall.

TINY. (*He grabs the suitcase and puts it on the desk in front of the screen.*) No. Don't bother. It's only a pair of pajamas.

MAYOR. Exactly. It's only a pair of pajamas. After everything you've done for us, it's the least I could ... That reminds me. I almost forgot the most important thing. For you. (*Hands him an envelope.*)

TINY. What's this? Ah, I understand. You know I never believed any of those stories about political payoffs...(*Chuckles, and the MAYOR chuckles with him.*)

MAYOR. And you shouldn't start believing them now, because this is not a bribe.

TINY. No. Too bad.

MAYOR. What a character. Always ready for a good laugh.

TINY. (*Bitter.*) Yep. That's me.

MAYOR. (*Still admiring.*) Do you think we'd insult a man of your reputation by offering you a payoff?

TINY. (*Disappointed.*) No, of course not.

MAYOR. (*Moving along unaware.*) This is the money that we've raised for the monument to Man's Best Friend.

TINY. (*In falsetto.*) What? (*Jumps to his feet.*) I think I've heard that name before.

MAYOR. Of course you have. The monument to man's best friend, his faithful dog. Don't you remember we wrote to you because of your special interest in animal rights?

TINY. Yes, yes. Now I remember. The monument to the faithful dog, man's best friend. Uhhuuuu ... (*Barks.*)

MAYOR. That's a damn good imitation. Sounds like a real dog.

TINY. (*Not amused.*) That's enough, please. (*Points to the envelope.*) How much is there?

MAYOR. Fifty thousand. Five thousand for the monument, and the rest for the new dog pound.

TINY. (*Feigning sincere interest.*) Why, do you want to build a dog pound?

MAYOR. Yes. Unfortunately, the old one burnt down and you have no idea how many strays there are in our town.

TINY. (*Rhetorical.*) Yes. So all you need is a little gas chamber, and ... Uhuuuu... (*Makes a gesture of exterminating dogs.*) Zac... Death to the strays, and a monument to the faithful. (*Puts his hand on the MAYOR's shoulder.*) Bravo. I'm glad you thought of coming to me.

MAYOR. (*With pride.*) There's no need to sign for it. We know our money's in good hands.

TINY. How right you are.

MAYOR. (*Leading him out.*) After you.

TINY. Where are we going?

MAYOR. To get the pajamas.

TINY. (*Taking big steps out the door.*) Yes, I might as well take the pajamas too.

(*They go out and lock the door. After a few seconds a key is heard in the lock.*)

ANGELA. (*Coming in, followed by the SENATOR.*) Here we are ... See what a beautiful room it is. Look at that big, soft, wonderful bed. (*She caresses it.*) You know I didn't close my eyes all night. Every time I was about to fall asleep, I'd remember how good it felt to be in such a luxurious bed, and I wanted to make the night last longer. So I turned on the light, splashed a little water on my face, and kept myself awake. I was as happy as a lamb.

SENATOR. (*Feeling sorry for her.*) You know, I've met some real looney tunes in my line of work, but you are ...

ANGELA. Look who's talking. A guy who runs around in his pajamas chasing a half naked train conductor ... I wish I had a picture of the doorman's face when he saw you.

SENATOR. (*Angry, hysterical.*) Stop it.

ANGELA. (*Mortified.*) Okay, I'll stop it. That's the thanks I get for pulling you out of this mess ... if the Senator who took your place hadn't been a friend of mine, you'd still be ...

SENATOR. (*Sarcastic.*) Don't make me laugh. Your friend ... Don't think that just because I'm fool enough to trust you, everyone else will too. If he was nice to you, it's probably only because of that stupid idea of passing yourself off as my wife. (*He notices his suitcase.*) My suitcase. They found it. (*Takes the suitcase and puts it on the bed.*) And since he believed you, who knows what he thought of me.

ANGELA. (*Sits on the sofa, gets up, sits on the armchair, gets up, goes to sit on the table where she finally feels comfortable.*) Don't worry. I didn't tell him that I was your wife. And as for being nice to me, he was always nice ... even before he became successful ... because he isn't all wrapped up in himself the way you are ... and if you want to know the truth, he even asked me to marry him.

SENATOR. (*Rummaging through the suitcase.*) Bum. (*Pulls out a nightshirt.*)

ANGELA. Well, not exactly to marry him, but he asked me to try and stay with him. But like an idiot I said no ... and ended up saying yes to you. Goddammit.

SENATOR. (*Sure of himself.*) There's still time to change your mind, if you want.

ANGELA. (*Melancholy.*) But who knows if he's still interested. (*With a hopeful smile.*) When he gave me the medals, it seemed like he was. (*Sinking back into melancholy.*) But in a position like his ...

SENATOR. (*Mocking her.*) He's probably thought it over, and ...

ANGELA. (*Missing the irony. Speaking as before.*) No. As long as he was playing Rigoletto, we might have been able to ... but now that he's come so far ...

SENATOR. (*Cutting.*) What. You never told me you worked in the opera.

ANGELA. (*Lashing back at him in the same tone.*) No? That's where I learned to play La Traviata.

SENATOR. (*Surprised for a moment by her irony. Resuming his cutting tone.*) Now that we've established your illustrious origin, I'm going to go and take a bath ... And to prove that you're not entirely useless, would you be kind enough to sing something for me. If nothing else it will keep me from falling asleep in the tub. (*The SENATOR's words leave ANGELA cold. He goes into the bathroom. She makes faces at him through the door like an angry child. The SENATOR keeps talking from inside the bathroom.*) Well? Did you lose your voice? Come on. Say something. Tell me about your true love. Ha. Ha. You know what I think: that you're imagination is getting the best of you: a Senator from Washington comes to take my place and his name is Sunny Weather, an ex-baritone who's madly in love with you ... what a whopper ...

Ha.Ha. Senator Sunny Weather... I'd like to meet him.

(*The sound of running water is heard.*)

ANGELA. (*Stays quiet for a moment, and then gets an idea. She goes to the door and knocks on it. Then she starts acting out a scene in a loud voice with the pauses and sing-song intonations of an amateur actress.*) Who's there? ... What? ... Oh, it's you Sunny ... No, dear, don't come in. I'm not alone. Go away, he's in the bathroom ... You want to talk to me? Okay, come in, but only for a minute. (*She opens and shuts the door, slamming it several times to be sure it is heard. She walks across the room stamping her feet heavily on the floor.*) Don't make such a racket, dear. He'll hear you. What are you doing? (*Mimes a passionate embrace.*) What's got into you, hugging me like that? Let me go, Sunny, let me go. You want a kiss? No, I can't. He might hear us. (*She kisses her hand.*) Oh no ... (*She slaps her hand.*) Excuse me for slapping you, but I had to do it. (*Imitating the voice of a man.*) No, no, no ... "Yes." (*She kisses and slaps her arm and hand repeatedly until she gets confused and slaps herself in the face.*) Oh no. That's enough. Sunny, please .. No go. (*Imitating the voice.*) "Come away with me"... "I can't." ... (*She turns towards the bathroom hoping to see the SENATOR lean out.*) Let me go. You're tearing my dress (*Imitates with her mouth, the sound of cloth ripping.*) Ripppp. Look, you've ripped it. What? You'll buy me another one? All in white? (*Goes towards the bathroom door. Raises her voice.*) "Yes." A wedding gown? ... "Yes." ... You want to marry me? (*Makes a mistake and gets the voices confused.*) "Yes." Then I'll come with you... Wait for me downstairs. (*She realizes her mistake and tries to correct it.*) I'll get my things and come down right away. Goodbye my love ... "Ciao, sweetie pie." (*She kisses her hand and slaps it again.*) Oh, excuse me. Force of habit ... Goodbye. (*Opens the door, then closes it again. In the meantime the SENATOR has appeared. He watches her, amused, as he dries his hair. She feigns surprise.*) Oh, its you.

SENATOR. (*Mocking her.*) Yes, it's me.

ANGELA. (*Feigns embarrassment.*) It was, uh ... room service ... the waiter ...

SENATOR. The waiter? A waiter named Sunny?

ANGELA. (*Still acting.*) Oh my God. You heard everything? But I swear I didn't mean to ... the door was open ... I couldn't stop him from coming in. (*She opens the door, behind which is revealed another door, the second of the double doors.*)

SENATOR. Yes, that one was open, but the other one?

ANGELA. (*Tries the door, but it won't open.*) It's locked?

SENATOR. (*Bursts out laughing.*) Ha. Ha. Yes, it's locked, and it's always been locked. I locked it myself ... and here's the key. So how did your beloved get in. Through the keyhole? Ha. Ha. What people won't do for love. In any case you have my compliments. It was a nice performance. My compliments and my thanks for the entertainment. But now calm down and be good while I write a few letters that I have to send out tomorrow. You can go to bed and turn off the light if you want. I'll sit here. (*He goes behind the screen, sits at the desk, lights a small lamp. A shoe thrown by the girl hits one of the screen's panels. The SENATOR snickers.*) I think I heard some one knocking, dear. Why don't you open the door?

ANGELA. Very funny. (*A noise is heard in the keyhole. The door to the room opens behind ANGELA. TINY enters, but ANGELA is leaning over behind the bed retrieving her shoe, so she doesn't see him. When she realizes it's him she whispers.*) Sunny, how did you get in?

TINY. (*Happy.*) Angela, I'm so happy you came back. I thought you'd run off with the Senator.

ANGELA. (*Pushing him.*) Quiet. He's behind there.

TINY. He's sleeping there?

(*The SENATOR snorts and tilts his head, convinced that ANGELA is play acting again.*)

ANGELA. (*Still whispering.*) No. He's writing letters, but you should leave before he hears you.

TINY. (*Also whispering.*) No way. I'm not leaving unless you come with me.

(*The SENATOR stops writing for a moment, listens for a moment, then begins writing again with a self satisfied smile.*)

ANGELA. (*Moved, embraces him.*) With you? ... Oh, Tiny, do you really mean it? (*She kisses him on the cheek.*)

TINY. (*Touches his cheek in shock.*) Angela, a kiss? (*He kisses her, and she slaps him.*)

ANGELA. Oh, I'm sorry ... it's just a reflex ... I'm getting all emotion. (*TINY hugs her so hard, he almost suffocates her.*) No. No. Don't squeeze me so hard. You'll tear my dress ... Look you've torn it. ...

TINY. I'll buy you a new one.

SENATOR. (*Without stopping his writing, trying to imitate TINY's voice, convinced it is still the girl acting the two voices.*) All in white.

ANGELA. Did you say all in white?

TINY. No, I didn't say all in white, but if you want a white one, I'll buy you a white one.

ANGELA. But how can we get out?

TINY. The same way I came in. I have the key. (*He shows it to her.*) Let's go. (*ANGELA grabs her suitcase, TINY helps her and also takes the SENATOR's which is on the bed.*)

ANGELA. It's too bad we can't take that beautiful bed with us too.

TINY. We'll come back for it later. Now, its enough just to be able to take you... (*They exit.*)

SENATOR. (*Happily singing the wedding march.*) dum-dum-de-dum ... dum-dum-de-dum. (*He applauds.*) Bravo. Bravo. Have you finished your heartwarming melodrama ... Ha. Ha. But that's enough for now. You're starting to get carried away. (*Folds his letter and puts it into an envelope.*) The first one was almost believable, but the second time, you really over did it. The male voice was so phony ... strictly amateur ... and then after I'd just finished telling you that I had the key, you made the same mistake again ... how were you supposed to get out, under the doormat? Ha. Ha. (*He leans out from behind the screen.*) Angela, where are you? Come on, stop playing around, come out ... I know, you're in the bathroom. Come on, don't tell me you're angry ... After all, you were joking too. Weren't you? (*Opens the door to the bathroom.*) No, not in there. Where are you hiding? (*Look under the bed.*) Stop kidding around, Angela.

(*The door opens and the MAYOR walks in.*)

MAYOR. (*Not seeing the SENATOR who is leaning over to look under the bed.*) Senator, here's the pajamas. Senator.

SENATOR. (*Standing up, distracted.*) Yes?

MAYOR. (*Surprised, in an accusing tone.*) Excuse me, who are you?

SENATOR. (*Angry, arrogant.*) What do you mean, who am I? I am ... (*Looks around.*) But, how did you get in here?

MAYOR. (*Obviously.*) Through the door. It was open ...

SENATOR. It was open? (*Goes towards the door and opens it.*) It's open!

MAYOR. (*Looking suspiciously.*) Would you mind telling me what you're doing in the Senator's bedroom?

SENATOR. (*Becoming crazed.*) But if it was open, and you didn't open it ...

MAYOR. (*Challenging him, coming closer.*) Will you answer my question? Who opened the door?

SENATOR. (*Letting himself fall into an armchair.*) That's what I'd like to know.

MAYOR. (*Slapping the back of the armchair.*) That's enough. Where is the Senator?

SENATOR. (*Without moving.*) Here I am. What do you want?

MAYOR. (*Slaps the chair again.*) Stop playing the clown. Where is the Senator?

SENATOR. (*Jumps to his feet. Points his finger at the MAYOR.*) Leaving aside the clown remark, which is worthy of a libel suit in itself, what Senator are you talking about?

MAYOR. The Honorable Senator Sunny Weather.

SENATOR. (*In a choked voice.*) Sunny Weather?

MAYOR. (*Rapidly, annoyed.*) Yes, the one who's staying here with his wife ... who seems to me to be more like his lover ... but what does it all have to do with you?

SENATOR. (*Flabbergasted, speaking like a ventriloquist.*) Senator Sunny Weather? ... Then he really exits?

MAYOR. (*Opens his arms.*) And why shouldn't he exist. Thank heaven he exists. He's the best Senator there is. (*Changes tone.*) But where is he?

SENATOR. (*Feeling the loss.*) He's run off with my girlfriend. (*Notices that his suitcase is gone.*) ... and my suitcase too.

MAYOR. (*Amused.*) Aha. It was his lover. Good for him.

SENATOR. (*Voice in his head, tearful.*) Left again without my pants!

MAYOR. (*Snickering.*) I can't say I'm sorry, because I do find you a bit unpleasant.

SENATOR. (*Looks at the MAYOR and gets an idea. Grabs the letter opener from the desk and point it at his goal.*) I want those pants.

MAYOR. (*Flustered.*) But ... why ... What are you doing?

SENATOR. (*Grabs the MAYOR from behind with a shoulder lock, still threatening him with the letter opener.*) Take off those pants or else ...

MAYOR. Okay, okay. I'll take them off. But, please, don't ruin my political career.

SENATOR. Your political career is a joke. Ha. Just give me those pants.

(*The MAYOR takes off his pants, and gives them to the SENATOR. Suddenly the CONDUCTOR runs in, still in his underwear, sees the pants, grabs them, and runs out.*)

CONDUCTOR. (*Barks like a dog.*) A man's best friend is his pants.

BLACKOUT

MUSIC

ACT III

Scene 2

*The lights go up. The curtain/fence is closed.
The actors are positioned as they were in the first
Act in the scene which proceeded the wedding.
The action resumes exactly at the point in which
the four friends notice that TINY has fainted.
TINY is still on the ground. One of his friends is
slapping him. The gentleman who we knew as the
priest is sitting at the table, just as he was in that
moment in the scene. The lights come up slowly
and a series of muffled sounds accompany
TINY's awakening.*

VOICE OF ANGELA. (*Coming from the void,
as if it were suspended in the air.*) Did you see, did
you see the look on their faces.

TINY. (*Speaking in his dream.*) Ha. Ha.
And look at that conductor run!

VOICE OF ANGELA. (*As before.*) Come on,
we can run too. Come on.

TINY. (*Still in the dream, moving his arms
slightly, his eyes still closed.*) Wait for me,
Angela. Angela, wait for me.

FIRST FRIEND. He's still dreaming.

DOCTOR. Throw a little water on him. That'll wake him up.

(*One of his friends sprays him in the face with a seltzer bottle. TINY gasps, opens his eyes, and looks around.*)

TINY. Angela ... Angela ... Where's Angela? (*He sits up and continues to look at this friends in disbelief.*)

FIRST FRIEND. (*Slapping him.*) It's about time. You had quite a snooze.

SECOND FRIEND. (*Passing his hand in front of TINY's eyes.*) Hey, wake up. You had us scared for a while. ... You were delirious, you kept talking and talking ...

THIRD FRIEND. And not only talking. You were barking too. ... Uhuuu....

(*They all laugh.*)

TINY. (*Very sad.*) So it was only a dream?

DOCTOR. (*Holds out a hand to help him up.*) Yes, and you were babbling about it for a full fifteen minutes. We were on the verge of calling an ambulance ...

TINY. (*Violently pushing away the hand of his friend.*) Goddamit to hell. It was a dream ... But it's not fair ... It's too easy to end a story that way ... When you don't know what to do next, you stop everything and say it was only a dream.

(*Still seated, kicks the DOCTOR.*) Son of a bitch, idiot, liar ... (*Short pause.*) Ugly bastard! I should have guessed. Just the fact that everyone had your faces, should have made me realize it was a dream. Goddammit to hell, ugly bastard, idiot ... (*Another pause.*) and son of a bitch.

(*All laugh.*)

DOCTOR. Come on, Tiny. Stop cursing, and give us a chance to cheer you up. While you were taking your nap, we prepared a little surprise for you: guess who this is. (*They all move away to reveal the new arrival.*)

TINY. (*Jumping to his feet.*) Impossible No. It can't be him.

FIRST FRIEND. Calm down. It's not the pastry shop owner.

TINY. I know, it's the priest.

(*They all look around at one another.*)

DOCTOR.
Yes, but how did you know?

SECOND FRIEND. Maybe he heard us while he was sleeping ...

THIRD FRIEND. Don't be silly.

TINY. (*As if in a spell, walks towards the phony priest, touches him, and then almost screams:*) You're alive?

PRIEST. (*In the same tone.*) Why, do you wish I weren't?

TINY. (*Ecstatic.*) Dear priest, did my friends bring you here for my wedding?

PRIEST. (*Entering his character.*) Yes, my son ... but calm thyself and be good.

TINY. (*As if he's gone mad.*) Kind priest, you're wonderful. Good priest, you're spectacular. Dear, dear, priest. (*Kisses his hands and slaps his vigorously on the back.*)

FOURTH FRIEND. (*Grabs him by the arm and tries to calm him down.*) Heave you gone mad? Tiny what's wrong with you?

SECOND FRIEND. He's flipping out. His head has gone into permanent "tilt."

TINY. (*Breaks free and lifts up his arms ecstatically.*) Quiet, guys. It's a replay.

THIRD FRIEND. What do you mean, a replay?

TINY. (*Whispering, as if he is afraid to break the spell.*) Don't you understand. We're going back to the beginning ... It's like in the movies. After the coming attractions, they show you the whole film again from the start. "The show must go on."

(*The FRIENDS look at one another with worried expressions.*)

FIRST FRIEND. He's over the edge.

TINY. (*Embracing the PRIEST again.*) Only this time the show is real. (*Stops suddenly.*) Wait. I didn't fall asleep again, did I? (*Hits a FRIEND who is standing nearby.*)

FIRST FRIEND. (*Surprised.*) Hey ... Oh!!

TINY. (*Takes his hand and shakes it warmly.*) Thank you. That means I'm awake. And if I'm awake and he's the priest, pretty soon we'll get to the part of the show where Angela comes in ...

DOCTOR. Who told you her name was Angela?

TINY. Her name is Angela. It's true! ... (*In a head voice.*) Great. ... Come on, Priest, let's get rolling ...

PRIEST. (*As TINY lifts him up onto his shoulders.*) Hey, what's got into you?

TINY. What's got into me? Tradition! I'm supposed to carry my wife's priest in my arms. Isn't that what you said. Forward march, men. Carry me to my blonde ... I swear that if she's the one I've been dreaming about, I'm going to hold her in my arms and never let go. (*They march in formation as before.*) Come on. Let's sing!

(*They exit singing in chorus: "Squeeze my wrists tightly."*)

ACT III

Scene 3

The Girl's Room. As in the Third Scene of the First Act, TINY and the Blonde stand, with their wrists bound, in the center of the room. His eyes are blindfolded. Her face is completely covered by a veil. The Priest has come to the end of the ceremony.

PRIEST. (*In a nasal chant.*) My blood will flow through your heart and yours will flow through mine, and we will be united as one, till death do us part.

ALL. (*In a chorus, including the GIRL.*) Till death do us part.

TINY. (*Euphoric.*) Yes, yes ... that's her voice ... she's the one ... oh I'm shaking all over ... I can't take it anymore.

PRIEST. You are now man and wife. Untie them, and let them see each other.

TINY. (*Electrified.*) Yes, yes ... let us see each other ... take this blindfold off ... (*Two FRIENDS help to untie them.*) Come on. Hurry up ... Wait. Let me take off her veil myself ... (*He rips the blindfold from his eyes and begins to take off the GIRL's veil, but stops with his hands in mid-air.*) It's you. It's you ... Just as beautiful as the one I dreamt about ... Even the same dress, the same veil ... (*His hands tremble.*) No I can't do it ... My fingers are jumping as if they were playing a harmonica ... Somebody else take it off. (*Points to the veil, which is still on the GIRL's face.*)

(*Two FRIENDS reach out their hands. The GIRL moves away.*)

BLONDIE.   No. Don't move. I'll take it off myself. I don't want you to ruin my hairdo.

TINY.   Come one. Hurry up. My eyes are going to pop out of my head. (*Then BLONDE takes off her veil, and reveals herself to look something like a marionette: a long and ugly nose, a thin masculine mouth, eyes hidden behind thick glasses, and bushy eyebrows that join together over her nose. Everyone laughs. Unable to hold themselves back.*) Nooooo! (*He stands petrified.*)

DOCTOR.   (*Pushing him towards the ugly creature.*) Is that all you have to say. What do you think of you new wife? We picked you a winner, didn't we?

TINY.   (*Shouting.*) Quiet, you shit faced bastards! (*Grabs the first one he can reach by the collar, and almost strangles him.*)

DOCTOR.   (*Trying to get out of his grip.*) No ... Let go ... let go... you dimwit ...

FIRST FRIEND. (*Trying with the others to free the DOCTOR.*) Take it easy.

SECOND FRIEND. (*Punching TINY, who doubles over in pain.*) What a spoil sport. And after we fix him up with a beautiful girl like that.

THIRD FRIEND. (*Throws TINY across the table. TINY responds by kicking him in the stomach.*) You're already married, pal. It's too late to kick up a fuss now.

FOURTH FRIEND. (*Jumps on TINY's back, grabs him by the neck, and slams him violently against the left wall.*) Are you going to calm down now. Come on. Don't act like this in front of you new bride. Go ahead, apologize ...

TINY. (*Panting, trying to compose himself.*) Excuse me, but I've got nothing against you. If you're not beautiful, it's certainly not your fault. It's just that these sons of ... (*Short pause.*) You're a professional, so I'm sure you understand. (*Walks downstage.*) But most of all, I'm fed up with whomever's in charge of manufacturing dreams. (*Almost speaking to the balcony.*) I want to know who's got that job.Which one of you archangels is it. Gabriel? ... Michael? ... Rapheal? ... Who is it ... (*He speaks as if he sees each one of them in the theater.*) Speak up, you archangels. If it's true what they told me when I was a child, that the Lord put you in charge of dream-making, why did you have to come and pick on me? ... Giving me dreams with double meanings ... why? ... Now I'm going to start screaming such filthy curses that you'll have to plug up your ears with corks ... Because if we can't even believe in our dreams any more ... (*Shouting.*) ... then there's nothing left ... it's the pits ... it's the god awful shit in the hole pits ... (*With a tense voice.*) What the hell do you think I am. A goddamn pinball machine that you can put your money in and bang around to make yourselves feel important?

(*They all laugh, but without much conviction.*)

PRIEST. (*Trying to break the tension.*) Come on, guys. We're missing our chance to kiss the bride.

FIRST FRIEND. (*Shouting euphorically.*) Yes. Yes. Let's kiss the bride. Me first ...

BLONDIE. (*Freeing herself violently from the PRIEST who held her by her shoulders.*) That's enough. Stop it. (*She takes off her glasses, fake nose and false eyebrows, revealing the beautiful face that we know so well.*) A joke is a joke, but he's right. This is the pits and I think it's disgusting ... You're not better than a bunch of wild baboons. Look what you've done to him. He's shaking like he's got the DT's.

TINY. (*Who has had his back to the GIRL, turns suddenly, sticks his neck out in shock, swallows.*) Angela.

DOCTOR. (*Goes to sit down lazily at the table.*) Now she's ruined everything. And the pea-brained whore wants to pontificate about it besides.

TINY. (*Touches his face with his hands.*) Angela, I'm dreaming again. (*Goes towards the DOCTOR.*) May I? (*He hits the DOCTOR. The DOCTOR responds by hitting him back harder.*)

DOCTOR. Hey. What are you mad at me for?

TINY. Ahi. (*Dazed, he supports himself on a chair.*) No, I guess I'm really awake ... (*Goes back to the DOCTOR and gives him a blow that sends him flying across the ground.*) That's for the "pea-brained whore."

BLONDIE. (*Coming to him.*) Thank you...

TINY. (*With great tenderness.*) Thank you...

BLONDIE. That will teach them to respect you. Do you know what I think. That even though they make fun of you, you're better than all those creeps put together ... Excuse me for playing along with them, but if I'd known that you were so...

TINY. So ... what?

BLONDIE. Well ... what can I say? I feel like I already know you ...

TINY. (*Lost in his vision of her.*) Of course you know me already. This is a continuous showing. Haven't you figured that out yet?

SECOND FRIEND. (*With real affection, putting his hand on TINY's shoulder.*) Hey Tiny, now that you've seen what she really looks like, you're not cursing anymore.

THIRD FRIEND. How could he? He looks like he's been mummified.

TINY. (*Suddenly he is in the center of the group, turning around looking at them like Samson among the Philistines.*) Stop it ... or I'll throw you all out of here ... (*Plays the conquering hero to the GIRL.*) See how I shut them up. (*They all blow him a big raspberry in a chorus. He pays no attention.*) Listen, I don't have to watch the whole film again from the beginning ... Let's skip the slow parts and get to the good stuff ... I already know how it's going to end. I know that your name is Angela, that your father knew all about plants and poles ... I'm your pole. Say yes, so we can run the credits and say goodnight.

BLONDIE. (*After a long silence.*) Yes.

TINY. (*Surprised.*) What?

BLONDIE. I said yes.

TINY. Yes, that we'll stay together...? Nooooo.

BLONDIE. Yes.

TINY. Oheuuu.

PRIEST. Come on gang, it's time for the violins.

(*All of them make a circle, miming an entire gypsy orchestra. It is all to the tune of "Squeeze My Wrists Tighter." TINY and BLONDIE don't notice them. They continue to talk and look at each other as if they were the only ones in the room. The gang and the girls continue*

to imitate in subdued tones the sounds and the
gestures of violin players.)

TINY. Well, if you can say yes that quickly
with no second thoughts, then ... (*Looks up.*) Hey
archangels, I'd like to apologize for what I just
said. I should have guessed that you wouldn't joke
around like that ... How could I imagine guys
like you making fun of people ... I always knew
that archangels don't play pinball ... I should
have trusted you ... You do a hell of a good job
making those beautiful dreams. Better than
Hollywood.

BLONDIE. (*Sweetly.*) Hey, Tiny, come down
to earth. What should we do? We can't very well
spend the night in this gypsy camp.

TINY. You're right. We should throw them
out, or leave ourselves. Let's get on a train and go
... go ... go. All we need is some money.

BLONDIE. Oh, I have some ... (*Goes towards
the dresser on the right.*)

TINY. (*Stopping her.*) No... No ... I've got a
whole envelope full of ... (*Reaching into his
jacket.*) How stupid. That was in the dream.
(*Stops with his hand at the level of his inside
jacket pocket.*) Eh. Is it possible? ... (*He puts his
hand inside his jacket and pulls out an envelope.
Rolls of hundred dollar bills are sticking out of
it.*) It's here.

(*Everyone is dumbfounded.*)

FIRST FRIEND. Holy cow. There must be thousands in there.

TINY. (*Again looking up at the roof of the theatre.*) Eh, no, archangels. Now you're going too far. You're trying to embarrass me, humiliate me. First you help me to find her, and now all this money ... No, I can't accept it.

(*By now all of the FRIENDS are also looking up at the ceiling in shock.*)

DOCTOR. (*Whispering, panting.*) Take it you idiot ... it's real ...

THIRD FRIEND. (*Touching the bills that are sticking out of the envelope.*) Hey, Tiny, remember that I've always liked you, and that I've always been you're friend...

ALL. (*Reaching out their hands.*) Me, too. Me, too.

PRIEST. (*Clearing them away.*) Me, too.

TINY. (*Nose to nose with him.*) I beg your pardon. I don't even know you... And with all this business about the gas chamber ... you're really starting to get on my nerves. (*Everyone looks at the false PRIEST with scorn.*) Nothing. Nothing for anyone. (*He opens his arms to get some breathing room.*) Before I'd give any of you a single dollar, I'd throw it all out the window. (*With three leaping steps he moves to the window, opens it, and throws out the envelope.*)

FRIENDS. (*Desperate, they catch up to him.*)
What are you doing, you fool ...

DOCTOR. (*Leaning out the window.*) The
idiot really did it. He threw all the money out into
the street...

PRIEST. (*Opens the door to the stairway and
rushes out.*) Come on down. Maybe we can get
some of it before it blows away.

(*The FRIENDS trample each other in a mad rush
to the exit.*)

WOMAN. Let me by.
FIRST FRIEND. Hurry.

(*All of them run downstairs. Only ANGELA and
TINY remain.*)

TINY. Aren't you going down with them?
BLONDIE. (*Quietly.*) No.

TINY. (*Slightly anxious.*) And now that I
don't have any more of that bankroll, do you still
want to stay with me?

BLONDIE. Well, I'm sorry you did it, and I
think you're crazy ... but I said yes before ... (*She
offers him her hand.*)

TINY. Ha. Now I can pull out that bankroll.
Again. (*He pulls a packet of money out of his
pants pocket.*) Oopla. ... Count it please.

BLONDIE. Ehou ... But how did you do it?!

TINY. It's a trick I learned from them. (*He points to the ceiling, and shouts at the top of his lungs.*) Archangels, you're the greatest. (*He takes ANGELA by the hand and runs away with her off the stage.*

MUSIC

CURTAIN

Other Publications for Your Interest

LLOYD'S PRAYER
(LITTLE THEATRE—COMEDY)

By KEVIN KLING

3 men, 1 woman (1 man & 1 woman play various parts). Bare stage w/set pieces.

Be amazed! The author of the amazing *21A* has fashioned a hilarious comic parable about Bob, the Raccoon Boy, and what happens to him when he is "rescued" from the raccoons who raised him and taught what it means to be human. At first, Bob can only make whirring raccoon sounds, but he is taught to speak by a delightfully whacko "Mom and Dad". He is taken from his cage at Mom and Dad's house by an ambitious ex-con named Lloyd, who sees the raccoon boy as his ticket to fame and fortune. When his first idea—displaying Bob as a carny sideshow freak—fails, Lloyd gets the brilliant idea to become a religious evangelist, displaying Bob as another sort of freak: a miracle from God. Lloyd's pitch, a promise of inspiration "that will bring grown men to a sitting position and women to a greater understanding of themselves", makes them both celebrities. By this time, Bob speaks pretty well ("I've been called many things in my life . . . But I prefer 'Bob'"), and is on the verge of innocence corrupted when there appears on the scene a beautiful guardian angel, dressed as a high school cheerleader. "Be amazed!", she declares, admonishing Bob to beware of Lloyd. What ensues is an amusing tug-of-war between the angel and Lloyd, with Bob the Raccoon Boy as the rope. The unqualified hit of the Actors Theatre of Louisville 1988 Humana Festival, this brilliant new comedy is "a whirlwind of original humor that comes in waves."—Lexington Herald-Leader. "Fresh, funny and charming."—Columbus Dispatch. "Kling is quite simply a comic genius."—Dramatics Magazine.

(#13997)

(Royalty, $50-$40.)

21A
(ADVANCED GROUPS—COMEDY)

By KEVIN KLING

1 man—Bare stage w/chairs.

"Astonishing", was the way Newsweek Magazine summed up this one-man tour-de-force in which Mr. Kling performed all the riders on a Minneapolis city bus: eight characters, including the driver. Structured as a series of monologues which in "real life" are going on simultaneously, this hilarious and decidedly "different" play had them rolling in the aisles at Louisville's famed Humana Festival where it won the prestigious Heideman Award. Kling started with the droll driver and moved on to such odd-balls as Gladys, Chairman Francis (a religious proselytizer), Captain Twelve-Pack (a drunk with a beer 12-pack box over his head) and a businessman who is decidedly *not* "Dave", no matter how fervently Captain Twelve-Pack insists that he *is*. And: who is the mysterious intruder sitting at the back of the bus? "Stunning."—U.S.A. Today.

(#22237)

(Royalty, $35-$25.)

Other Publications for Your Interest

CINDERELLA WALTZ
(ALL GROUPS—COMEDY)
By DON NIGRO

4 men, 5 women—1 set

Rosey Snow is trapped in a fairy tale world that is by turns funny and a little frightening, with her stepsisters Goneril and Regan, her demented stepmother, her lecherous father, a bewildered Prince, a fairy godmother who sings salty old sailor songs, a troll and a possibly homicidal village idiot. A play which investigates the archetypal origins of the world's most popular fairy tale and the tension between the more familiar and charming Perrault version and the darker, more ancient and disturbing tale recorded by the brothers Grimm. Grotesque farce and romantic fantasy blend in a fairy tale for adults.

(#5208)

(Royalty, $50-$35.)

ROBIN HOOD
(LITTLE THEATRE—COMEDY)
By DON NIGRO

14 men, 8 women—(more if desired.) Unit set.

In a land where the rich get richer, the poor are starving, and Prince John wants to cut down Sherwood Forest to put up an arms manufactory, a slaughterhouse and a tennis court for the well to do, this bawdy epic unites elements of wild farce and ancient popular mythologies with an environmentalist assault on the arrogance of wealth and power in the face of poverty and hunger. Amid feeble and insane jesters, a demonic snake oil salesman, a corrupt and lascivious court, a singer of eerie ballads, a gluttonous lusty friar and a world of vivid and grotesque characters out of a Brueghel painting, Maid Marian loses her clothes and her illusions among the poor and Robin tries to avoid murder and elude the Dark Monk of the Wood who is Death and also perhaps something more.

(#20075)

(Royalty, $50-$35.)

Other Publications for Your Interest

KNOCK KNOCK
(LITTLE THEATRE—FARCE)

By JULES FEIFFER

3 men, 1 woman—Composite interior

Take a pair of old Jewish bachelor recluses, throw in Joan of Arc who also in another life was Cinderella—add another character who appears in various guises and you have the entire cast but not the story of this wild farce. Cohn, an atheistic ex-musician is the house-keeper "half" of this "odd couple." Abe, an agnostic ex-stockbroker is the practical "half." They have lived together for twenty years—are bored to tears with one another and constantly squabble. Cohn, exasperated, wishes for intelligent company and on the scene enters one Wiseman who appears in many roles and is part Mephistopheles, part Groucho Marx. Then Joan of Arc appears before the couple telling them her mission is to recruit two of every species for a spaceship trip to heaven. After that all antic hell breaks loose and continues to the mad ending. "... a wild spree of jokes ... helium-light laughter."—Clive Barnes, N.Y. Times. "... a kooky, laugh-saturated miracle play in the absurdist tradition."—Time. "... grand fun, possessed by a bright madness ..."—N.Y. Post. "... a knockout of original humor."—NBC. "... intelligent and very funny play."—WABC-TV.

(Royalty, $50–$35.)

LITTLE MURDERS
(ALL GROUPS—COMEDY)

By JULES FEIFFER

6 men, 2 women—Interior

"Jules Feiffer, a satirical sharpshooter with a deadly aim, stares balefully at the meaning-less violence in American life, and opens fire on it in 'Little Murders.' ... Can be devas-tatingly lethal in some of its coldly savage comic assaults." (N.Y. Post). The play is really a collection of what Walter Kerr called set pieces, showing us a modern metropolitan family of matriarchal mother, milquetoast father, normal cuddly sister, and brother who is trying to adapt himself to homosexuality. Sister's fiance is a fellow who knows how to roll with the punches; he figures that if you daydream while being mugged, it won't hurt so much. They have a hard time finding a preacher who will marry them without pronouncing the name of God. But they succeed, to their sorrow. For immediately afterward sister is killed by a sniper's bullet. A detective who has a stack of unsolved crimes suspects that there is "a subtle pattern" forming here. "'Little Murders' is fantastically funny. You will laugh a lot."—N.Y. Times. "You have made me laugh, you have made me collapse. I want to go back."—N.Y. Post. "One of the finest comedies this season.—NBC-TV.

(Royalty, $50–$25.)